Enlarged and Revised Edition

ATHLETIC INSTITUTE SERIES

JUDO

By
Sadaki Nakabayashi
7th Dan
Henry Okamura
5th Dan

Hikaru Nagao
5th Dan
Dr. Paul V. Harper
3rd Dan

Morey Korey
1st Dan

STERLING PUBLISHING CO., INC. NEW YORK
Oak Tree Press Co., Ltd. London & Sydney

ATHLETIC INSTITUTE SERIES

Baseball	Judo
Basketball	Junior Tennis
Girls' Basketball	Table Tennis
Girls' Gymnastics	Tumbling and Trampolining
Gymnastics	Wrestling

Fifth Printing, 1974

Copyright © 1968, 1967, 1961 by
The Athletic Institute
Published by Sterling Publishing Co., Inc.
419 Park Avenue South, New York, N.Y. 10016
British edition published by Oak Tree Press Co., Ltd., Nassau, Bahamas
Distributed in Australia and New Zealand by Oak Tree Press Co., Ltd.,
P.O. Box J34, Brickfield Hill, Sydney 2000, N.S.W.
Distributed in the United Kingdom and elsewhere in the British Commonwealth
by Ward Lock Ltd., 116 Baker Street, London W 1
Manufactured in the United States of America
All rights reserved
Library of Congress Catalog Card No.: 68-18804
Sterling ISBN 0-8069-4316-5   Oak Tree 7061 2050-7
            4317-3

Table of Contents

1. The Sport of Judo 5

2. Breakfalls 24

3. The Art of Throwing 49

4. Additional Throwing Techniques 71

5. Mat Techniques 96

6. Offensive and Defensive Mat Techniques 125

    Seiri-Undo 152

Index 158

Primitive combat

1. The Sport of Judo

In every region of the world, there is some form of unarmed combat which has sprouted from primitive roots. Through the years, geographical and cultural influences have shaped these forms of combat into the contact sports we know today. Boxing and wrestling are present-day, Western-world developments of unarmed combat.

In Japan, a form of unarmed combat emerged which is more than a contact sport. It teaches not only contest proficiency, but develops the mind and the body—following a strict moral code. It is a sport, a physical culture, a philosophy, known as Judo, "the gentle art."

Judo was developed by Professor Jigaro Kano. At the age of 18, the professor began a long, intensive study of Jujitsu—an ancient method of unarmed combat practiced by Japanese

Two contestants

Beginning a match

warriors. "Not only did I find Jujitsu interesting, but I also realized it was most effective for the training of both body and mind. So by taking together all the good points I had learned of the various schools and adding my own inventions and discoveries, I devised a new system for physical culture and moral training . . . as well as winning contests." This is how Professor Kano described the birth of Judo.

Along with nine students, he established the Kodokan school in Tokyo in 1882 to develop the science of Judo. Today, Kodokan Judo is practiced all over the world. The Kodokan actively directs techniques, safety, and instruction of Judo wherever it is practiced.

Judo, though evolved from Jujitsu, is not intended to be a crippling form of combat. It is a sport—to be studied and played according to the rules and ceremonies of the Kodokan. Kodokan translated means: "A school of studying the 'way'." The "way" is the practice of using maximum efficiency and minimum effort to overcome an opponent. This book is an introduction to the "way."

As a Judoka, or Judo player, you must know how to wear the Judo uniform. This uniform, or Judogi, is composed of three pieces—trousers, jacket, and belt.

The trousers, made of heavy cotton, are reinforced at the knees and have a loop at the waist. They are loose-fitting and should extend at least halfway between your knees and ankles.

After you have put on the trousers, pull the drawstring out sideways to tighten the waistband.

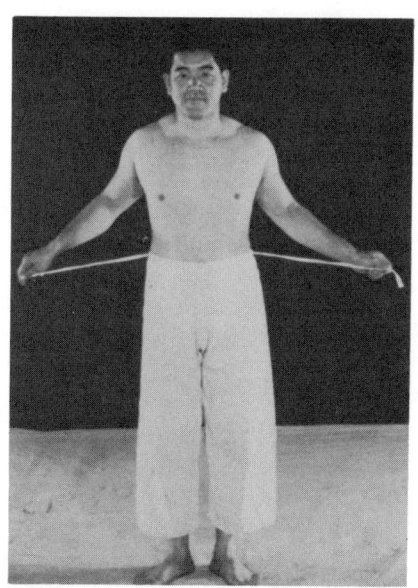

Pass one end of the draw-string through the loop of the trousers, then pass the other end through the loop. Tie the ends of the draw-string into a bow knot.

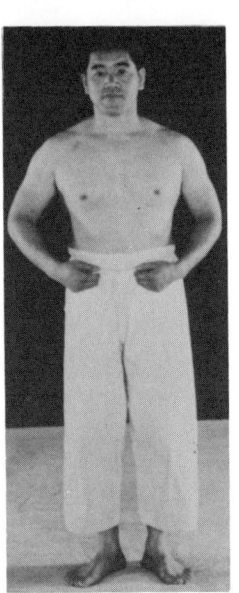

Now, put on the jacket and bring the right side loosely across the body. Cross the left side of the jacket over the right side so that the lower edge is parallel with the waist. The sleeves of the Judogi are loose-fitting, and should extend halfway between the elbow and wrist.

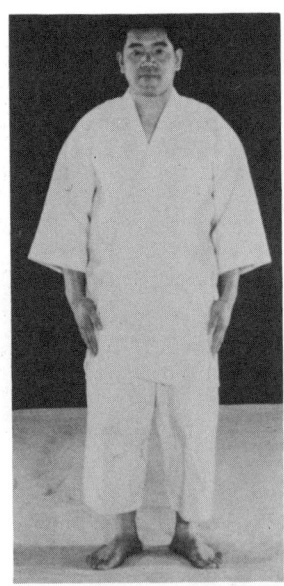

The Judogi belt should be long enough to encircle your body $2\frac{1}{2}$ times. First, grasp the belt in the middle and pass it around your waist from front to rear, so that it crosses in the middle of your back. Next, bring both ends around to the front.

Cross one side of the belt, either right or left, over the other at the waist. Tuck the end of the belt, which is in front of the crossover, under both loops. Now tie both ends into a loose square knot. Tighten the knot by pulling both ends of the belt. This completes your dress.

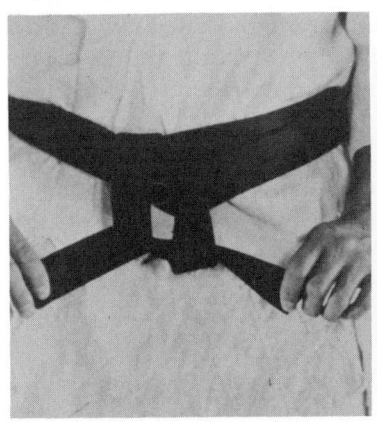 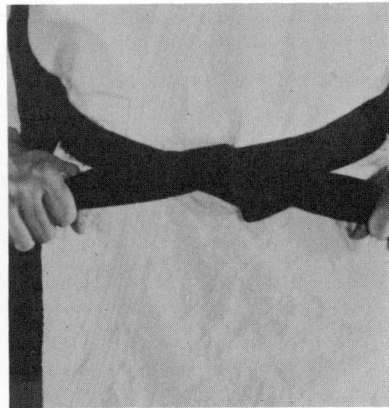

Watching the Judoka

The Judo hall is a place for culture. You must conduct yourself in a serious manner at all times. Idle banter and noisy actions have no place in Judo practice or training. Even when you are not on the mat your fullest energies should be directed to those who are exercising. Good manners are as much a part of Judo as the execution of proper offensive and defensive techniques.

One of the most important ceremonies in Judo is the salutation, or bow. This is not just a greeting; it is a demonstration of your respect for your opponent and should be made seriously before and after all practices and contests.

Upon entering or leaving the Dojo or gymnasium where you practice Judo, you come to a brief halt and perform a Tache-Re. At the edge of the mat, you again bow, facing inward. The Tache-Re is also performed upon leaving the mat and before and after each workout with a partner or opponent.

The Tache-Re is performed while standing about 6 feet from your partner or opponent. In class, or during a workout, it is accomplished by common consent. In a tournament, however, this may be performed at the command "Rei" by the referee.

This is the proper posture for the Tache-Re. Notice the angle of the feet.

You bow from the waist, allowing your arms and hands to slide down and slightly forward. Direct your eyes forward and down.

Performing the Tache-Re

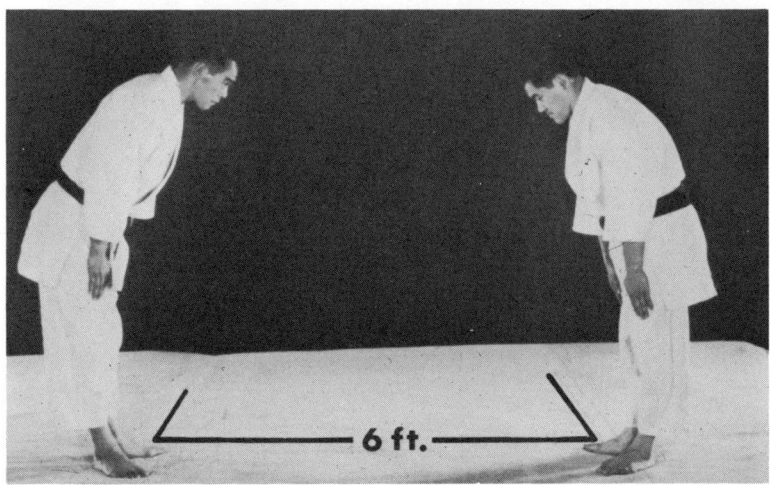

The Zarai, or sitting bow, is performed before and after each class period and Judo tournament. This salutation is done by all of the Judoka simultaneously.

You begin the Zarai from the standing position. Bring your left foot back and kneel, keeping the bottom of your toes on the mat. Your right hand is along your right thigh. Your left knee is in line with your right foot. Head and body are erect, eyes straight ahead.

Now, bring your right leg back, and place it alongside your left leg. Your body is erect, hands touching sides, knees parallel.

Beginning the Zarai

Front view

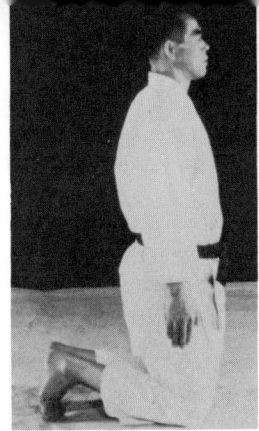 *Knees parallel*  *Sit back*  *Front view*

Reverse your feet and toes so that the toe-nails are facing *down*. Place the big toe of your right foot, over the big toe of your left foot. Sit back on your feet.

Bring both hands inward to the front of your thighs. Notice the distance between the knees. Now, without raising up, bow forward to a 45-degree angle. Bend your head down slightly but keep your eyes raised. Bring your hands down on the mat.

Right toe over left   *Side and front view of bow*

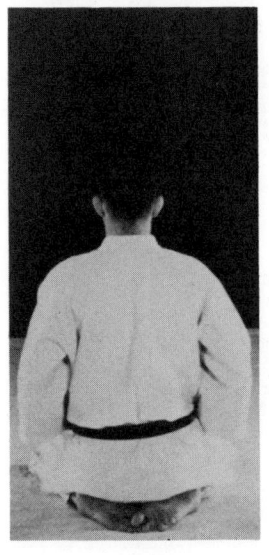

Hold the bow for a two count, then return to the sitting position. You stand up by reversing the same procedure you used to kneel.

The color of the belt worn by a Judoka denotes his rank. There are three ranks—white belt, brown belt and black belt. The black belt is the highest, white the lowest. There are three grades of the brown belt, and ten degrees of the black belt. The sixth, seventh and eighth degree black belt holders may wear a red and white sectioned belt, and the ninth and tenth degrees may wear a *solid* red belt. A Judoka may earn promotions in rank through knowledge, demonstrated ability of various Judo techniques, time in grade and competition in tournaments.

Three different belts

About to begin

Now that you know something of the history, dress, ceremony and rank of Judo, you are ready to begin practice. Before an actual Judo session, it is necessary to loosen your muscles and joints through a series of exercises.

These warming-up exercises are of vital importance to your own safety on the mat, because you are far less likely to be injured if your body is relaxed and flexible. Repeat each of the following exercises several times before each workout.

First, with your feet about 18 inches apart, swing both arms to the right side and left side. Allow your body to pivot freely on your hips.

Swinging and pivoting

 *Rolling the head*	 *Swinging the arms up*

To loosen your neck muscles, relax and roll your head in complete circles. Keep your eyes open. Alternate directions. Next, rock your head forward and back, then tilt it from side to side. Keep your chin forward and try to touch your ear to your shoulder.

Swinging down 	*Bending to the side* 

Swinging in a circle   *Loosening the knees*

Now, with arms extended, swing your hands upward and back, stretching as far as you can. Keep your head back.

Next, swing your arms forward and down so that your arms pass between your legs. Keep both legs straight. Straighten up and repeat the exercise, stretching a little more each time.

With your feet spread 30 inches, and without bending forward, slide one arm down your side to below the knee. At the same time, sweep your other arm upward in a circular motion so that it almost touches your head. You should feel the stretch from your heel along the entire side of your body to your fingertips. Reverse the exercise to the other side.

With feet 30 inches apart, hands raised, palms forward, and legs straight, bring your body and arms down in a circular motion, around the right side of your body. Follow across to the left side. Continue this sweeping motion until your arms are high above your head. As your body straightens up, stretch backwards as far as you can. Reverse the procedure from left to right.

To loosen the knee joints, bend forward (see above), legs straight, feet 18 inches apart. Press backward on both knees with the palms of your hands. Now drop into a squat position.

Squat position   *Stretching leg*

Keep your heels raised, knees pointed outward, and buttocks as low as possible.

To stretch your leg muscles, stand with your feet 30 inches apart, and parallel to each other. Bend one leg, knee pointed forward, and lower your body to a squat position with the weight centered over the heel of your bent leg. Simultaneously, *raise* the toes of your other foot, so that only the heel is in contact with the mat. Keep your leg straight and press on the thigh just above the knee. Without moving your feet from their position on the mat, stand up and reverse the action by bending your *other* knee forward.

For the next exercise, sit on the mat and grasp one leg just above the ankle. With your other hand, revolve your foot with a cranking motion to the right and to the left. Bend your foot forward and backward, and from side to side. Rub your feet briskly with both hands. Now shake your wrists vigorously and pop your knuckles.

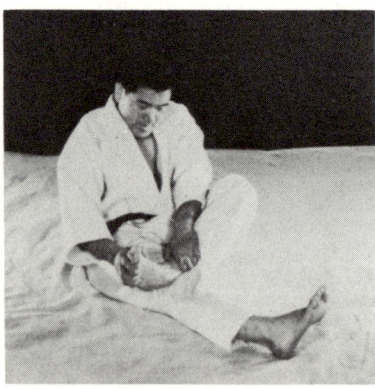

Loosening the ankle

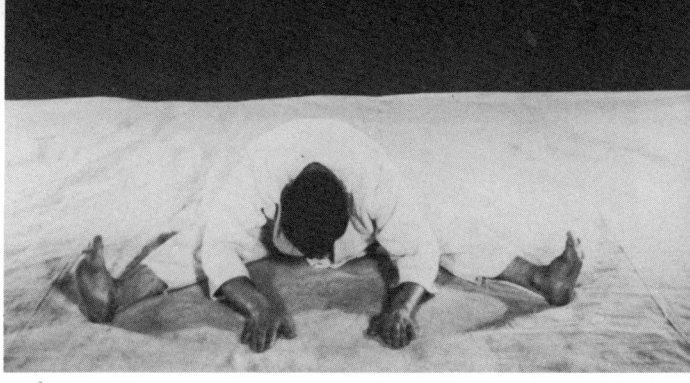

Stretching backs of legs

From a sitting position, spread your legs as far as possible. Reach forward and try to touch the mat with your forehead. Sit up and repeat the exercise. From the same position, touch each knee with your forehead several times.

Next, try several Judo push-ups. With your feet set wide apart, hands on mat at shoulder width, push *back* as far as possible. Lower your chin close to the mat and *arch* your head and body downward and forward, then up, until your body is supported by your toes and hands. Your chest and waist should follow the swooping arc of your head. Return to the first position by pushing up and back.

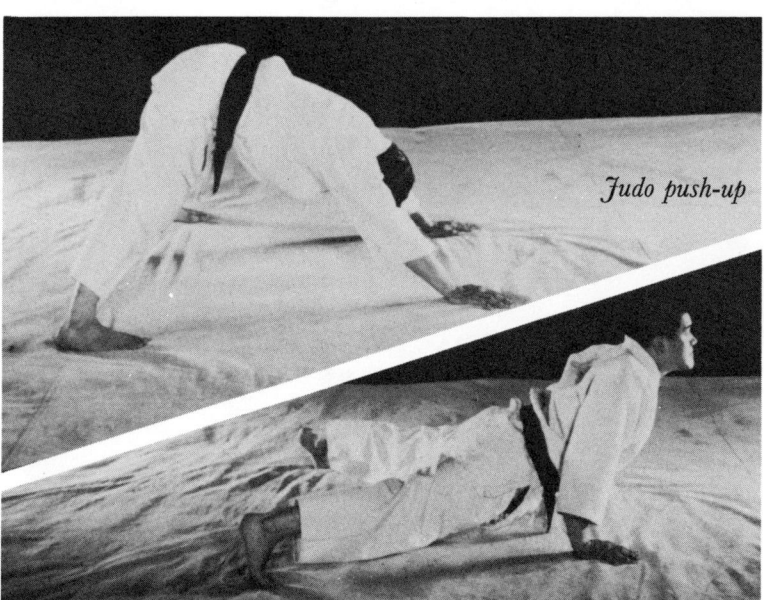

Judo push-up

Touching toes

Rocking on the back

In the sitting position with legs extended, reach forward and try to touch your toes or beyond them.

Next, bring your arms and legs up and over your head to the rear. The backs of your hands and big toes should touch the mat. Return to the sitting position and touch your toes.

Lie on your stomach and place your hands in the small of your back. Alternately raise your head and chest, then lower them and raise your feet and legs. Stretch as much as possible each time. Then, raise both head *and* legs and rock back and forth.

Rocking on the front

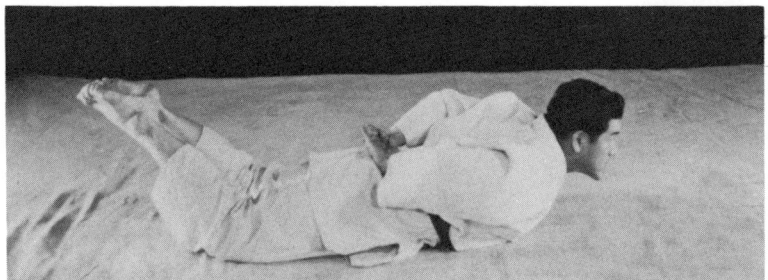

A push-up with a twist

Now, assume the position for a push-up. Bring your right leg under your left leg as far as possible, twisting your body to the right. Repeat the exercise to the left, concentrating on hip action.

Lie on your back, lift your head, raise your arms, and clench your fists. Bring your right knee back to your chest and *snap* your left leg forward. Keep your toes curled back. Reverse legs and repeat the exercise.

Snapping the left leg forward

The body bridge

The next exercise is the body bridge. Lie on your back and bring your arms up and back over your head so they are parallel to the mat. Bring your feet back as far under your buttocks as possible. Roll your head back and arch your body up, so that only your head and toes touch the mat. Keep your chin tilted up. Return to the first position by rolling your head forward and lowering your body.

This is similar to the body bridge. Assume the first position. As you bridge upwards, roll your head back and to the right. Twist your right hip and shoulder down. Swing your left arm up and to the right. Roll your head and body back to the starting position and repeat the exercise on the other side.

Body bridge with a twist

The back snake crawl

This mat exercise is called the back snake crawl. Lie on the mat, face up, arms close to your body, elbows at your hips. Pull your left leg back and bring your left foot close to your left hip. Push with this foot and scoot the body backwards. At the same time, twist onto your right side and bring your left arm across your head. Now, twist to the left side and repeat the exercise until you have moved 15 or 20 feet across the mat.

You will have to study and work hard before you have mastered these techniques, but the thrill of winning a Judo tournament is worth every minute of the work and practice.

2. Breakfalls

Beginning Judo requires a thorough knowledge of how to stand. Here is a Judoka, or Judo contestant, standing in the correct natural posture or Hon-Shizentai. Notice the relaxed, "comfortable" stance. The weight is evenly distributed—feet parallel about shoulder-width apart. Body erect. Knees relaxed. Eyes level.

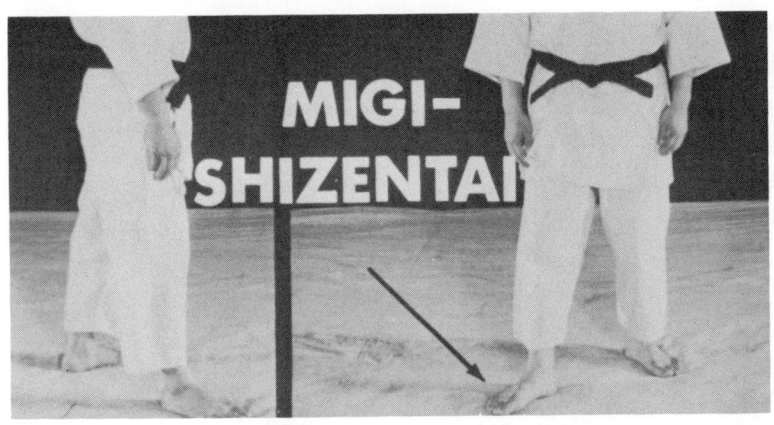

This is known as the right, natural posture or Migi-Shizentai. In this traditional Judo stance the right foot is extended slightly forward. The weight of the body is adjusted accordingly, to maintain equal distribution and balance.

This is Hidari-Shizentai—the left natural posture, which is the Judo stance with the left foot forward.

These then are the three basic Judo stances, known as "natural" postures: Hon-Shizentai, Migi-Shizentai and Hidari-Shizentai. Natural . . . right . . . and left.

While there are various places to grasp an opponent's jacket or Judogi during a Judo match, this is the basic grip.

The right hand clasps the opponent's lapel at the height of the armpit, while the other hand seeks and holds the sleeve just

Grasping opponent's jacket

below the bend of the elbow. This is the basic hold from the right natural posture. Because both men are employing the same hold—this view serves to illustrate the position of both hands.

The same basic hold from a left natural position calls for a reversal of hand positions as you see here.

Grasping with left hand

Moving forward

At all times during the course of a Judo match, or practice, the primary objective is to maintain balance and proper control of the body. In a hand-to-hand bout you must be ready to act instantaneously with perfect freedom. Therefore, when moving on a Judo mat, you must always strive to maintain a firm balance base. This is accomplished by moving forward in the manner you see here. One foot is advanced—the other is brought quickly up. Then the starting foot is moved forward again. The feet never pass each other as in ordinary walking. This rule applies to starts with either foot, and the same practice is religiously followed in retreating.

Moving sideways

In moving sideways, the same general principle holds true. The trained Judo player moves one foot out—the other follows just far enough to establish a balanced base. Then the starting foot is advanced again. The feet are never crossed, or brought too close together because these actions leave you momentarily awkward and vulnerable.

In turning right or left—whichever the case may be—the lead foot is advanced in a circular movement, while the ball of the other foot forms a firm pivot. In Judo, turns are known as

Tai-Sabaki and are widely employed in throwing an opponent in a manner like this:

Notice here how a turn to the left utilizes the whole body in the starting of a throw.

Just as the aim in a Judo match is to maintain balance and control of yourself at all times, one of the goals of offensive action is to upset the balance of your opponent. Breaking the posture of your opponent is known as Kuzushi.

O = Opponent

Beginning the throw

There are many ways of breaking your opponent's balance in Judo. In the upper left hand corner a pushing technique is used to break balance to the direct rear. In the upper right hand corner a sudden pull is used to break balance to the front corner. In the center, the opponent's balance is weakened by lifting or floating him to his toes. The bottom two scenes illustrate the upsetting of the balance to the left and to the right. Upsetting your opponent's balance makes it easier to execute the technique you have in mind—even when facing a stronger opponent—because loss of balance means loss of strength.

However, to take a closer look, the initial maneuvering for balance does not mean just pushing, or pulling, or lifting. Sometimes you "push" and then stop. Pull and suddenly loosen. Pull and then push. Push or pull from left to right with quick reverses. A skilful series of feints and pressures breaks your opponent's balance. These methods of Kuzushi are vital to "setting up" the opponent for the continuation of your attack.

Maneuvering the opponent

Before we get into the area of Judo techniques, however, proper caution and instruction demand that a study be made of Ukemi, the Judo art of breaking the fall. Ukemi enables a

Falling without harm.

Judoka to fall safely and easily. On the mat, Ukemi enables you to land without shock or injury when being thrown. It's also invaluable in lessening the effects of accidental falls in everyday life.

Ukemi is important to all the techniques of Judo, including the art of throwing. It is rightly said that the best way to learn to throw an opponent is to *be thrown* ten thousand times. Learning to break the fall effectively requires proper conditioning and perfecting of timing. Therefore, Ukemi training must begin with a series of simple exercises:

Step 1

From a prone position—head and shoulders lifted as much as possible, eyes directed toward the knot on the belt—raise your arms vertically to a position like the above (Step 1).

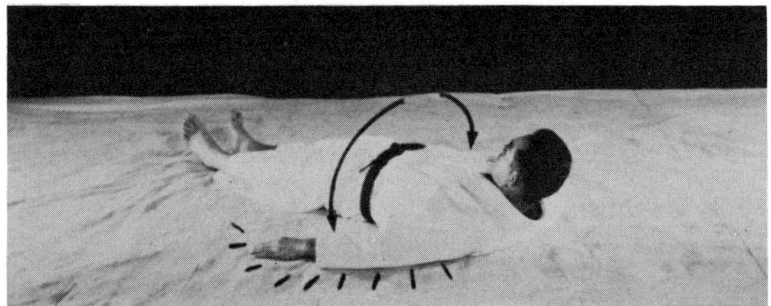

Step 2

Then, freely slap the mat with both hands and under forearms, bouncing them off the mat and directly up again (Step 2). This practice should be started slowly and cautiously. Gradually increase the tempo as your conditioning improves until you are striking the mat quite quickly and sharply.

Looking at the beginning exercise from a side perspective, direct your attention to the position of the head. It never

Side view

touches the floor. One of the main purposes of the breakfall is to keep your head from striking the mat. Therefore, throughout the course of these exercises it is vitally important that you keep your eyes fixed on the knot of your belt.

This is a sequence demonstrating side-to-side body rolling. Lying on your back, raise your head, shoulders and legs off the mat. Bring your right arm up and away from your body, palm outward (Step 1).

Roll over on your right side bringing both legs and your right arm down together, striking the mat as a single unit (Step 2). The outer edge of your right foot, the inner edge of your left foot, and the striking arm all break the fall simultaneously. At

Step 1   Step 2

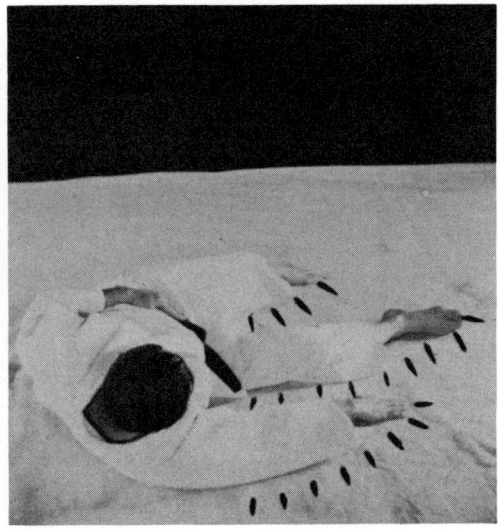

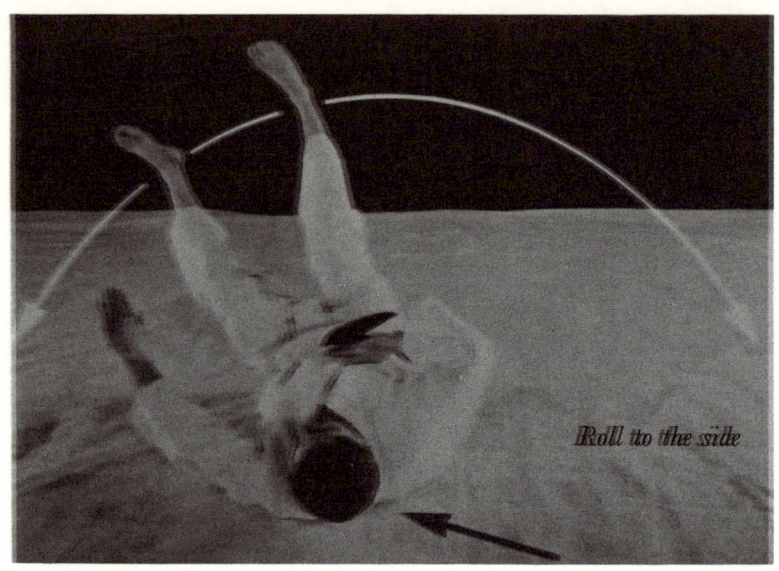
Roll to the side

the conclusion of the roll, both feet should be parallel and about waist width apart.

Without hesitation bring both feet up in a high arc and repeat the roll to the other side: one continuous action from side-to-side, without stopping. NOTE: Head and upper neck are off the mat at all times.

When you feel you are ready, the falling practice may be started from a sitting position. With legs extended, raise your arms to the front bringing them simultaneously over your head (Step 1). Then topple over backwards swinging your legs up in a generous arc (Step 2). Bring your arms downward in the

Step 1

Step 2

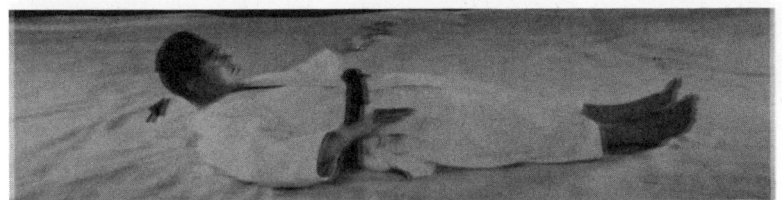

Side view

slapping motion learned, timing the action to beat the mat just at the moment your upper back makes contact.

At the end of the sequence note that your head and shoulders never touch the mat. Chin should be kept on your chest and your eyes should be trained on the knot on your belt. The action is continuous—at the completion of the backfall, you return without pause to a sitting position and then the backfall is repeated.

Ukemi from a squat

After you have mastered Ukemi from a sitting position you may advance to practicing the fall from a squat.

  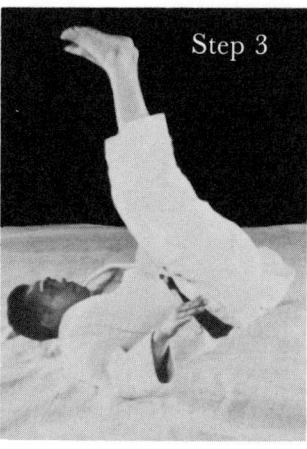

This is the sequence of action. With arms extended, fingers slightly overlapping, buttocks resting on your raised heels (Step 1), roll over backwards, raising your arms overhead (Step 2). Again, as your back makes contact, your arms should be brought down with a slicing motion to strike the mat just as your back makes contact (Step 3).

Then bring your arms up with a snap, and return to a squat position in one continuous motion (Step 4). In falling, remember to keep your buttocks close to your heels and *your head and neck up off the mat.*

Step 1   Step 2   Step 3

This is the sequence of the backfall from a standing position. With arms parallel to the floor (Step 1), start dropping your body by bending your knees and raising your toes. As you are lowering, raise your arms high (Step 2). Tuck your heels in close to your buttocks as in the fall from a squat (Step 3).

At the moment your balance is lost, your arms should be brought down sharply to strike the mat at the same time as your back makes contact (Step 4). Legs should be brought up and over in the follow-through. Chin tucked in. Head and neck off the mat. Keep your eyes focused on the knot on your belt. Allow your arms to snap up and off the mat at the finish of the arm beat. Rise and repeat.

Step 4

Step 1

Step 2

This is the beginning position (Step 1) for a sidefall from a sitting posture. Your legs are outstretched to the front, one hand resting easily and naturally on your thigh. Your striking arm is held across your chest in the manner illustrated.

Then roll to the striking hand side, raising the legs (Step 2), while at the same time striking the mat to break the fall. Keep your head and shoulders up off the mat. Allow the striking arm to bounce up after the blow. Arm and hand should be relaxed throughout the exercise. After completing the fall, allow your legs to drop and, sitting up, repeat the fall to the other side. Continue to alternate sides during the conditioning period.

Sidefalls from a squatting posture begin like this (Step 1). With your striking arm in cross-chest position, turn your opposite knee somewhat out (Step 2), and the leg on the falling side out to the front and across the body in the direction away from the fall.

Fall to your side, striking the mat with your arm and hand to break the fall (Step 3). Your body should land with your head and neck off the mat, your chin tucked in. Your legs are allowed to come up and follow through. Rising to a squat position, continue the exercise by practicing falls to either side, alternately.

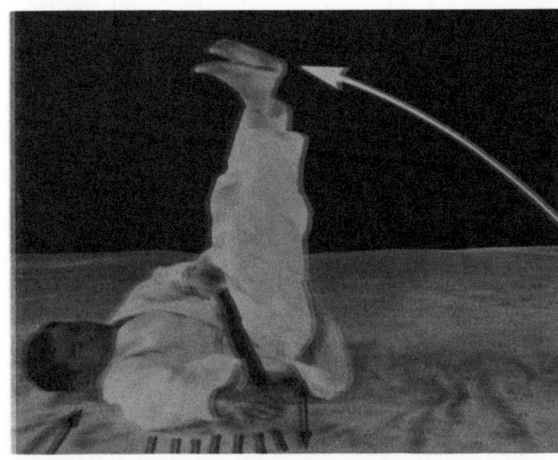

Step 1

The sideways breakfall from a standing position is similar to the squat, but from a higher level, both feet parallel. Bring your right arm downward and across your body to the left side (Step 1). At the same time throw your leg in a sweeping motion across your body. Bend your left knee deeply to lower your body. The hip should touch the heel as you roll.

Then bring your arm down hard, breaking the fall by striking the mat with your entire arm—from armpit to fingertips (Step 2). Allow the legs to come up in a follow-through. Rise and repeat to the left side.

You will sometimes need to perform the forward somersault: From a standing position advance your right foot one

Step 2

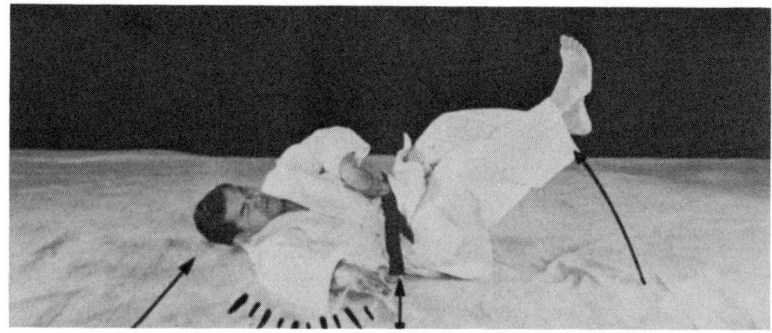

pace forward. Lower your body and place your left hand parallel with your right foot and in line with your rear foot to form a triangle (Step 1). Note the position of the fingers on the left hand—they point inward directly towards your right foot.

Step 1

Next, place your right hand on the mat, palm down, fingers pointing to the left foot (Step 2).

Step 2

Tuck your head in, turning your chin to the left. Using the rounded right arm as the outer edge of a wheel, roll over the arm and over the right shoulder (Step 3).

Step 3

Step 4

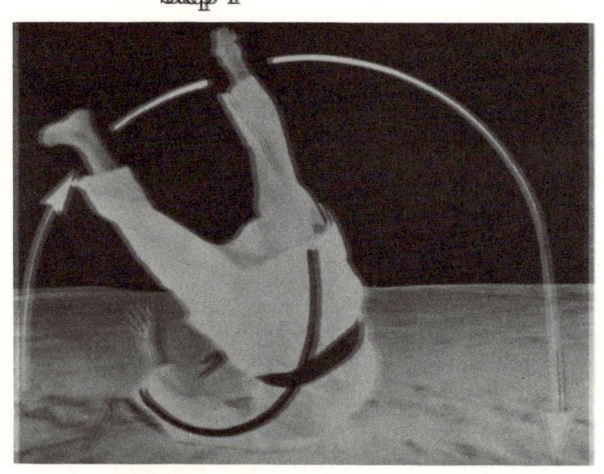

Bring both feet over in a big arc, rolling on an imaginary angle of a line running from your right shoulder to your left leg (Step 4). At no time does your head come in contact with the mat.

Just before the upper left of your body strikes the mat, slap the mat with your left arm to break the roll (Step 5). At the conclusion, your head and shoulders should be up off the mat—feet parallel. Practice this exercise by alternating left and right feet and hand positions.

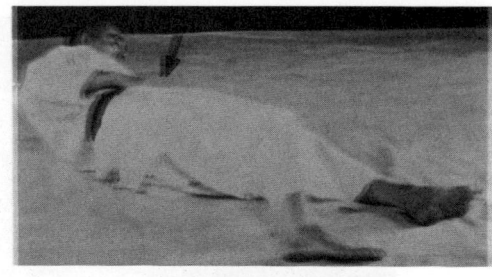

Step 5

The next rolling breakfall is the one-hand forward somersault. This is the same as the two-hand forward maneuver from a higher level, the left hand kept free from the mat. Again, as you follow this sequence, note the head and neck are kept up off the mat.

One-hand somersault

Diving breakfall

After you have mastered the one- and two-hand forward somersaults you continue to the diving breakfall: Take 6 or 8 running steps and dive in a running somersault over a fellow Judoka. As you become more proficient, add other kneeling figures to lengthen your dive.

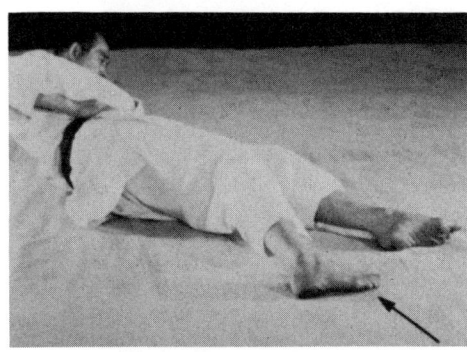

Ending in reclining position

All of the somersaulting breakfalls should be practiced in two different ways: (1) Ending in a reclining position and (2) allowing the momentum of your roll to carry you completely over and back to a standing position.

In falling forward from a kneeling position extend your arms horizontally (Step 1),

Step 1

and fall forward on your hands, fingers turned slightly inward (Step 2).

Just before your chest contacts the mat, turn your head sideways, so that it is parallel to the mat and not touching (Step 3).

Step 2

Step 3

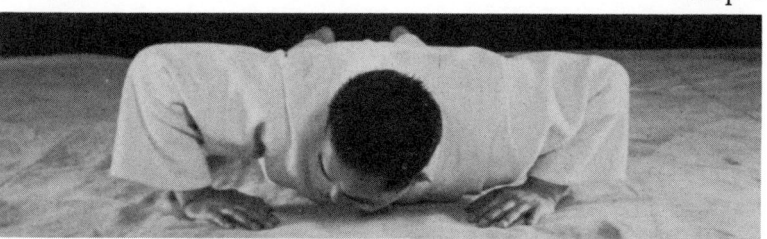

Falling forward from a standing position is much the same as from a kneeling position—make contact with the mat in the same manner. At the moment of contact with the mat only your hands and your toes touch the mat. Do not allow your knees or chest to touch until after contact has been made.

Beginning position

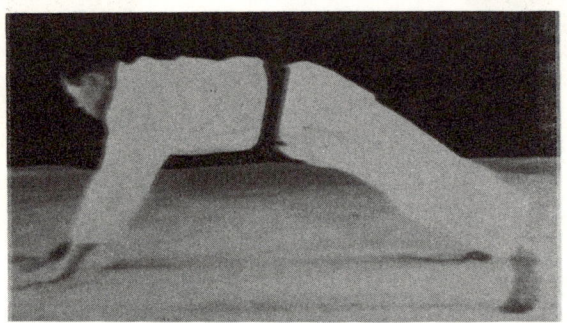

The fall

Learning to fall properly is a Judo *must*. Remember, "The best way to learn to throw an opponent is to be thrown ten thousand times." Knowing how to fall will give you the confidence you need to perform naturally—at your best—and truly enjoy "the gentle art."

3. The Art of Throwing

After learning to prepare and condition yourself for the vigorous sport of Judo, the next concern is Tachi-Waza or the art of throwing from a standing position. Tachi-Waza is divided into three categories: Te-Waza, or hand techniques, in

"O" identifies opponent

which the opponent is thrown mainly through the action of the thrower's hands (or the hands play a major role in the throwing), Koshi-Waza or hip techniques, in which hip action is the main feature of the throwing, and Ashi-Waza, *the leg and foot tech-*

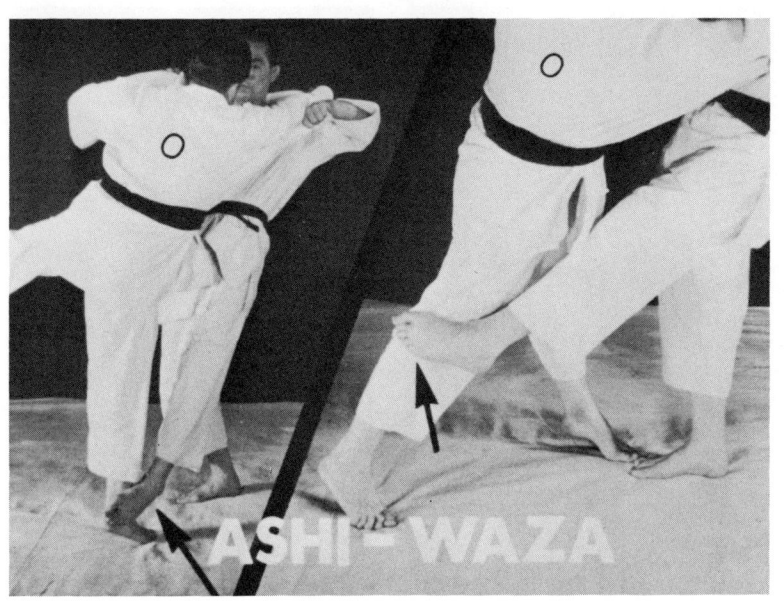

niques. (While the word "Ashi" in Japanese, literally means "foot," in Judo usage Ashi techniques include the entire leg from just above the knee as well.)

The leg and foot techniques are the dramatic Judo throws by which a small man is able to toss a much larger opponent with only a slight movement of the foot. They are said to be the essence of Judo technique. Ashi-Waza is the most scientific of the three general techniques and therefore requires deftness and precision timing which can come only from diligent practice.

One Judoka throws another

Step 1   Step 2

From a right natural posture we are going to describe De-Ashi-Harai, an advancing foot sweep, leg technique. Holding your Judo partner's lapel with your right hand, and his outer, middle sleeve with your left hand (Step 1), withdraw your right foot to your right back corner making your opponent advance his left foot.

At the same time, with your left hand pull on your opponent's right sleeve forcing him to advance his right foot in order to maintain balance (Step 2).

At the precise instant his foot is about to touch the mat, turn your left foot (Step 3) and apply the sole against your op-

O = Opponent

Step 3

ponent's outside ankle and right heel. Sweep his leg out from under him in a forward and inward direction (Step 4). At the same time, pull his right sleeve strongly down, completing the throw (Step 5).

Step 4

Step 5

Step 1

This is Hiza-Guruma, the knee wheel, to your opponent's right leg. From a right natural posture, bring your right foot back and to the right a half-step, turning your foot so that it faces your opponent's right heel (Step 1). At the same time lift upward on his lapel and pull on his right arm, breaking his balance to the right front corner. Then pull his left sleeve in an upward motion floating him on his left foot. Push up with your right hand; simultaneously bring your left leg up, knee straight, and gently place the sole of your foot against the outside front of his knee (Step 2).

Notice from the close-up photo that care should be taken, at time of contact, to *gently* place the sole of the foot against the knee. This is not a kicking or striking motion, which might injure your opponent—but a blocking action.

Pivoting on your right foot as much as possible, and continuing the twisting motion, throw your opponent over the blocking foot (Step 3).

HIZA-GURUMA

Step 1

The next throw is a knee wheel (Hiza-Guruma), too, applied to the leg in the right back corner. Starting from a right, natural posture, step back a full pace to your right rear, pulling slightly on your partner's left lapel, but loosely holding his right sleeve. This will cause him to take a step forward with his left foot (Step 1). Then relax the forward pull of your right hand, and suddenly reverse your pressure to a solid push against his left shoulder—pushing it back and around to the right rear, while, at the same time, pulling on the left sleeve to create a circular "steering" motion (Step 2). This will break his balance to the right front corner.

Bring your left leg up now (Step 3) and place the sole of your left foot, leg straight, on the side of his knee in a holding action.

Your opponent is thrown over your foot with an unbroken continuation of the steering motion (Steps 4 and 5).

O = Opponent

Step 2

Step 3

Steps 4 and 5

Step 1

Now we turn to the hip techniques. This is the beginning of Uki-Goshi—the floating hip throw. Starting in a right, natural position (Step 1), step back one pace—while pulling and lifting your opponent with your right hand on his left lapel, causing him to advance his left foot (Step 2). Then with your left hand, pull him slightly upward to make him float and break balance towards his right front corner.

Next, encircle his waist with your right arm and at the same time turn (Step 3), placing your right foot inside his right foot and moving your left foot back around in front and outside of his right foot—pulling him up snug.

Notice that your back must be kept straight. Solid contact must be maintained from hip to armpit by keeping erect and not leaning forward.

Throw him (Steps 4 and 5), twisting your hips from right to left.

Step 2

Step 3

Steps 4 and 5

Step 1

Step 2

To execute O-Goshi—the major loin throw—start from a right, natural position. Follow up by moving your left foot back one step (Step 1), forcing your opponent to advance his right foot to maintain balance; then, with your right hand, pull on his lapel, forcing him to bring his left foot parallel to his right. At this point, lift with both hands, floating him to his toes, breaking his balance to the direct front (Step 2).

Then, use your right arm to encircle his waist. Turn, placing both feet inside his (Step 3). Make solid contact with your right side from hip to shoulder. Bend your knees to bring your

O = Opponent

hip line below his belt. Straighten your knees—and with a twist of your hips from right to left, throw your opponent over your hip (Step 4).

Complete the throw (Step 5).

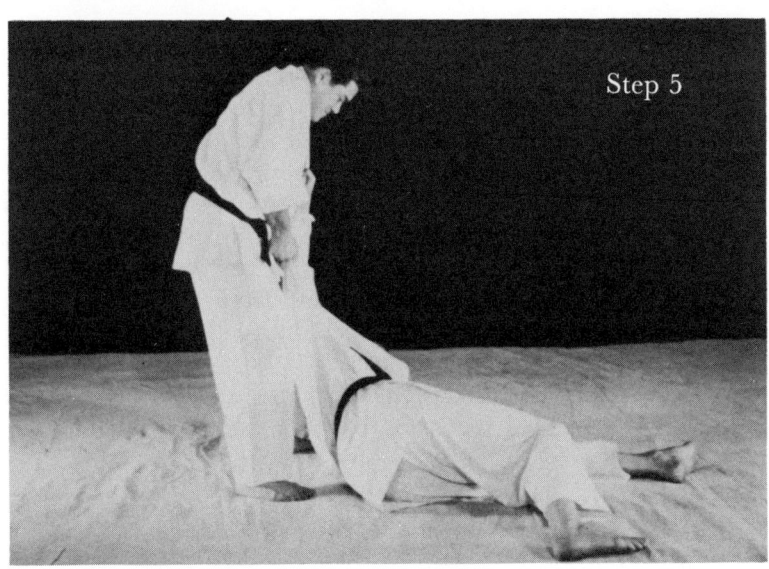

Step 1

Another foot technique, O-Soto-Gari—or major outer reaping—is one of the most popular contest throws. It starts from the right natural posture (Step 1).

Make your opponent step forward on his right foot by pulling him gently to his right front corner. Move your left foot to a point a little outside his right foot, and break his balance to the right rear corner by the combined action of both hands. Your left hand pulls in (Step 2), and your right hand pushes up and back (Step 3, a view from the other side). Notice the vertical position of the hand so that your forearm will come in contact with his chest.

With his balance broken in the right back corner (notice in Step 4 that his left foot is on his toes and all of his balance

Step 2

Step 3

rests on his right foot), raise your *right* leg and swing it forward and past his right leg. Then, suddenly "reap" or sweep back-

Step 4

Step 5

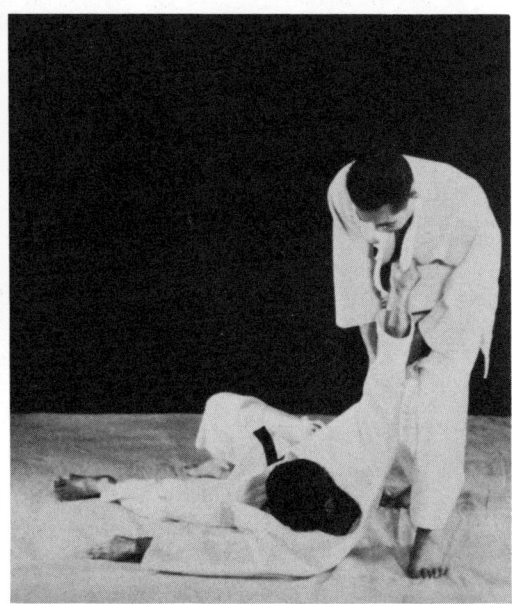

Step 6

wards and outwards near the middle of his right back outer thigh, making contact with the same region of your right thigh (Step 5). At the same time push with your right forearm, and your opponent will fall backwards. He will be thrown as in Step 6.

The next throw to be demonstrated is Sasai-Tsurikomi-Ashi, or propping-drawing-ankle throw. Beginning from a right, natural posture, advance with your left foot, and push with your left arm, forcing your opponent to step back on his right foot (Step 1).

"O" identifies opponent

SASAI-TSURIKOMI-ASHI

Step 1

By lifting and pulling with your right hand and at the same time pulling with your left hand, break his balance towards his right front corner (Step 2). Seize that moment to place the sole of your left foot against the lower part of his right leg

Step 2

Step 3

(Step 3). Simultaneously twist your body back and around to the left, pulling hard with your left hand on his right sleeve and pushing with your right hand on his left lapel (Step 4). He loses his balance and is thrown over your propping foot to his left side as in Step 5.

Step 4   Step 5

O-UCHI-GARI

Step 1

In performing O-Uchi-Gari, the major inner reaping, you first pull your opponent to the left front corner (Step 1).

You break his balance to the left rear corner and swiftly place the back of your right knee to the back of the knee of your opponent's extended left leg (toes pointed downward as in Step 2). Then reap it towards your right back corner, describing a big arc with your toes (Step 3).

Step 2

Step 3

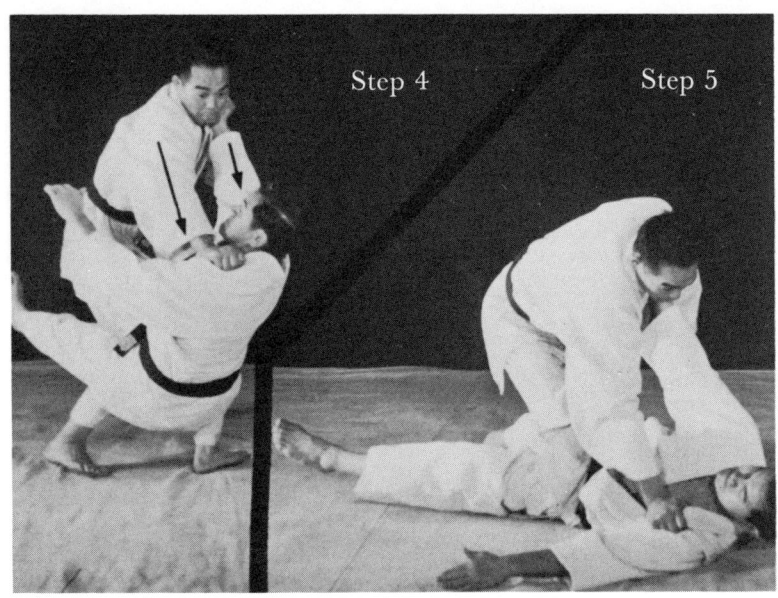

The fall is completed by pushing directly downward with both of your hands (Steps 4 and 5). All these movements are simultaneous, and co-ordinated. If properly executed, your opponent will fall directly backwards.

In Ippon-Seoi-Nage, the one-hand-over-the-shoulder throw from the right natural posture, step back one-half pace with your left foot. At the same time, draw your opponent forward and slightly up, causing his balance to be broken to the right front corner (Step 1).

Then, step *across* with your right foot, placing it just in front of his right foot. Then, bending your knees slightly and pivoting on the ball of your right foot, move your left foot back inside his left foot and hook your right elbow up under his right armpit (Step 2). Keep your back in close contact with his chest and abdomen, as you see in Step 3. Straighten your legs, bend your body forward and pull both arms downward.

Step 2

Step 3

O = Opponent

Step 4

Throw your opponent over your right shoulder, as shown in Step 4. The essence of Kodokan Judo lies in the refinement of throwing techniques. The beginning throws you have seen demonstrated are an introduction to the simple, scientific logic that forms the base for your entire Judo training. Learn them well because you will use them over and over again.

4. Additional Throwing Techniques

Step 1   Step 2

Because the throwing techniques represent the greater part of the abilities of a Judo player we shall continue the demonstration of throws in this unit, starting with Marote-Seoi-Nage, the two-arm shoulder throw. Step back on your left foot (Step 1) and pull your opponent's upper body forward (Step 2). The moment his balance is broken to the right front corner, or directly forward as you see in Step 2, advance your right foot to the inner side of his right foot.

Then pivot on the ball of your right foot, and place your left foot inside your opponent's left foot, as you see in Step 3a. Note: Your back and hip make a solid contact from his upper chest down to his thigh. It's important that your hip be snug to his thigh.

Step 3a

Step 3b

From a front perspective (Step 3b) notice your body must be perfectly parallel, directly in line with your opponent. Your right arm is bent at the elbow and under his right armpit—

O = Opponent

wrist locked forward. At this moment he is floating on his toes, while you are in a low posture, below his center of gravity.

Step 4

Step 5

Suddenly you straighten your knees, raise your loins, lean your upper body forward and throw him to the front over your right shoulder, completing the throw as you can see in Steps 4 and 5.

Step 1

This is Ko-Soto-Gari, the minor outside reap. Starting from a right natural position, pull lightly to the front with both hands—your opponent will pull back to retain his balance (Step 1).

Taking full advantage of his backward reaction, provide an additional force of your own in the form of a steering action with both hands, which shifts his balance to his heels, and his right back corner. You step to his right side (Step 2) and in one continuous motion you pull down with your left hand, push up and back with your right hand, and reap his right leg from under him with your left foot (Step 3a).

In a close-up of the action from the other side (Step 3b), notice the position of your foot at the exact moment of contact during the reap. Your reaping leg should be absolutely straight, and your foot turned to apply the sole flat against your op-

Step 2

Step 3a

Step 3b

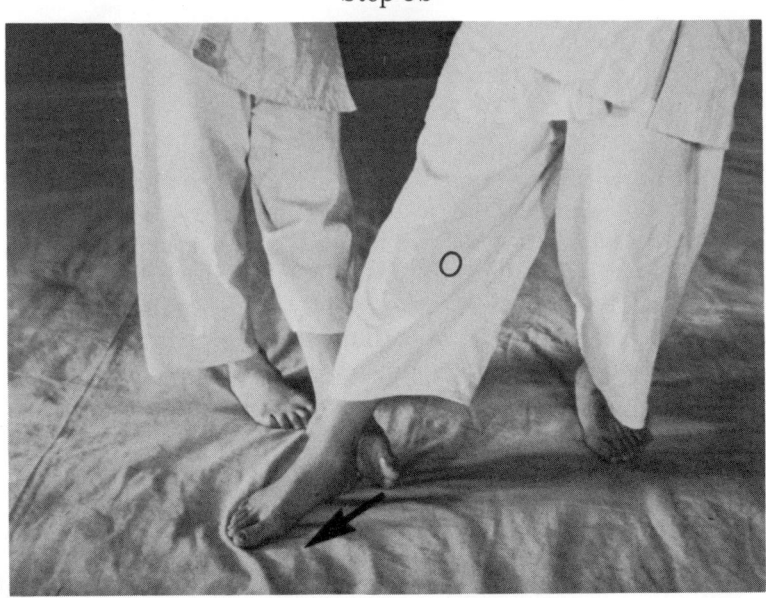

ponent's heel. Follow through in the direction shown. He will go down directly at your feet, as shown in Steps 4 and 5.

Step 4

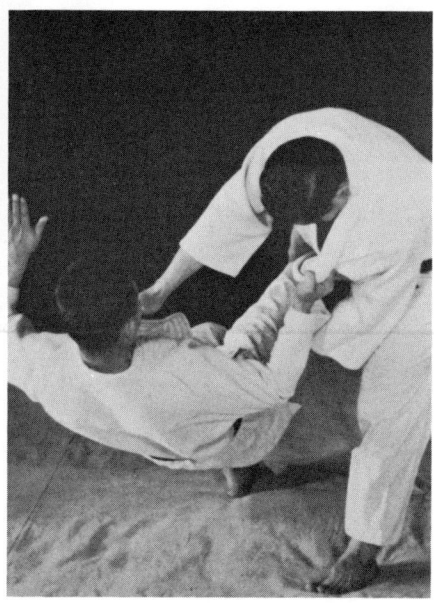

Step 5

Now, Ko-Uchi-Gari, the minor inside reap. From a right natural start, bring your left foot back and around as you see here. By pulling naturally on your opponent's right sleeve, and pushing his left shoulder down and back with your right hand, you will break his balance to the back left corner (Step 1).

As he advances his right foot slightly to maintain his stance, reap his right front leg from within with your right foot. Step 2 shows a close-up of the action from in front of his left leg. Pay particular attention to your leg, extended straight, and the way your foot, sole forward, cups and sweeps his right heel straight ahead in the direction of his toes.

O = Opponent

KO-UCHI-GARI

Step 1

Keeping your eyes directed towards the back of your right hand, press downward and back with that hand and forearm while your left hand pulls on his left sleeve. He will go down in his right back corner, as shown in Step 3.

Step 2

Step 3

The lift-pull-hip-throw

This is Tsuri-Komi-Goshi, the lift-pull-hip-throw. The first two words, Tsuri-Komi, refer to the beginning lift-pull action. The mastering of the lift-pull is important because it is a basic beginning for many of the popular contest throws. Goshi means hip. So this is the *lift-pull* action as it's used to set up *a hip throw*.

Begin stepping back with your left foot, while pulling up and forward on his right sleeve. Lift upward and forward on his left lapel and float him up, making him vulnerable on his toes (Step 1).

Pivoting on your right foot, with knees slightly bent, you swing around and place your left foot within his left foot. Draw him up snugly to your back with right elbow under his left armpit, body low, hip against his right thigh (Step 2a).

Step 1

Step 2a

In the front view of the position before the throw (Step 2b), note the firm grasp of your right hand on his left lapel, your

Step 2b

Step 3

left hand on your opponent's right sleeve. As he leans over your back, lift with your hips. As you straighten your knees you will push his thighs upward. Follow by twisting your body to the left, giving a pull with both hands. Your opponent will revolve over your hip (Step 3) and be thrown.

SODI-
TSURI-
KOMI-
GOSHI

This is Sodi-Tsuri-Komi-Goshi, the sleeve-lifting-pull-hip throw. This hip throw is essentially the same as the hip technique you have just seen. The difference? For greater leverage the lifting is applied to the sleeve rather than the lapel.

Start by switching your right hand from your foe's lapel to his left sleeve. Gripping his sleeve near the top of the elbow, slide your right foot near your left heel, and draw your opponent forward by pulling on his left sleeve (Step 1). Now step across with your left foot toward his left toes, with your knees bent. At the same time push his right arm straight upward (Step 2). The combined action of lifting his right sleeve and pulling on his left sleeve will float him to his toes.

Step 1

Step 2

"O" identifies opponent

Step 3

Step 4

Next, slide your right foot to the front of his right foot and complete the clockwise turning of your body, forming a solid chest and back contact diagonally down his body from armpit to left forethigh (Step 3). By lifting your opponent with your legs and hip, and turning your body from left to right in coordination with the movements of your hands, you complete the throw (Step 4).

OKURI-ASHI-HARAI

Okuri-Ashi-Harai, the sweeping ankle throw, is usually applied when the opponent is moving to the side. Starting from the right natural position as your opponent moves to his left, move in rhythm with him.

As he steps out to the left and widens his stance, before he can close the gap by following with his right foot, press his right elbow against his right side with your left hand. At the same time push—then pull—with your lapel hand to float him on the toes of his right foot (Steps 1a and b).

Step 1a

Step 1b

At that very moment, with your left leg well extended, sweep his right foot toward his left in much the same manner as the advancing foot sweep (Step 2). Following through with a counter-clockwise movement of your hands, sweep your foot

Step 2

Step 3

across and well beyond your right leg, throwing your opponent as shown in Step 3.

Step 1

This is the Tai-Otoshi, the body drop. It is a hand technique. From a right natural posture bring your left foot back and around in a semi-circle, simultaneously pulling on his sleeve in a wide arc. Your right foot remains pointing toward your opponent (Step 1).

Use both hands as though they were turning a steering wheel—pull with your left hand and forearm! Pushing with your right hand, palm down against his chest, wheel him

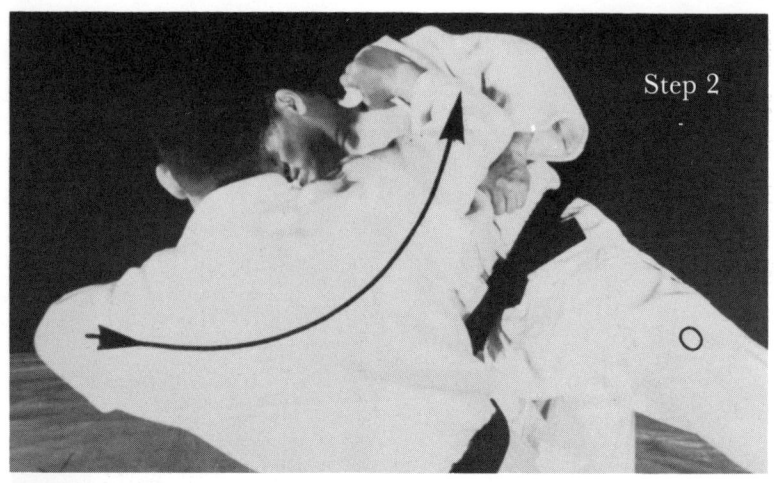

(Step 2) and thus break his balance to his right front corner (Step 3).

Then, pivoting on the ball of your left foot, swing around as shown in Step 4. Place your right foot past his right ankle in a blocking action with both knees bent.

O = Opponent

Step 4

Straightening your right leg with a snap (demonstrated in the upper left hand corner of Step 5) apply both your hands and body in a quick, twisting motion—throwing him over your blocking leg in a manner like this. (Note that his left arm, raised high, is in a perfect position to break his fall.)

Step 5

Step 1

The next technique we will cover is Harai-Goshi, the sweeping loin throw. In the usual start from the right natural posture, step back half a pace with your left foot and turn your right side to your opponent's direct front, at the same time exerting a forward and upward pull on his right sleeve. Meanwhile your right hand lifts and pushes in the same direction, lifting him to his toes and breaking his balance in the right front corner (Step 1).

Now, as you pivot on the sole of your right foot, bring your left foot back and around parallel to your right foot—in between and in front of your opponent's stance (Step 2). Your back turns to his front and you insert your right elbow and forearm under his armpit (Step 3).

Step 2

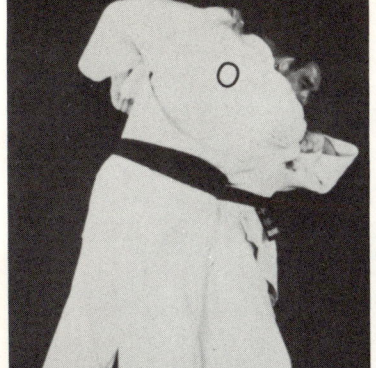

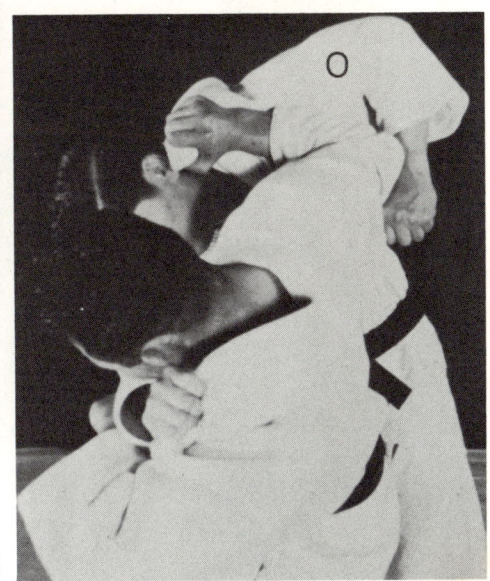

Step 3

Now, maintain solid leg contact between your own body and his front, from armpit to hip, and apply the back of your thigh—from calf to hip—to the front and outer side of his leg and thigh, with your toes pointed down and curled, leg straight (Step 4).

Step 4

Step 5 Step 6

By sweeping around, pushing with your right hand and pulling with your left, you will throw your opponent dramatically over your sweeping leg (Steps 5 and 6).

Uchi-Mata, the inner thigh throw, is the No. 1 contest throw. Move your right foot to a position where it points across the front of your opponent's toes, and at the same time lift upward with both hands. You will float him out of balance, as shown in Step 1.

As you pivot on your right foot, quickly skip your left foot back to the position you see here. Then with one continuous motion you swing your right leg between his legs (Step 2).

O = Opponent

Step 1

Step 2

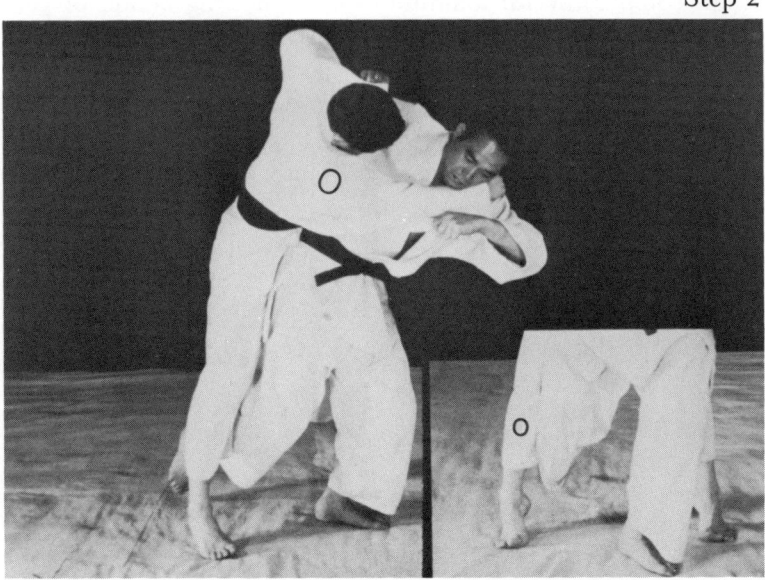

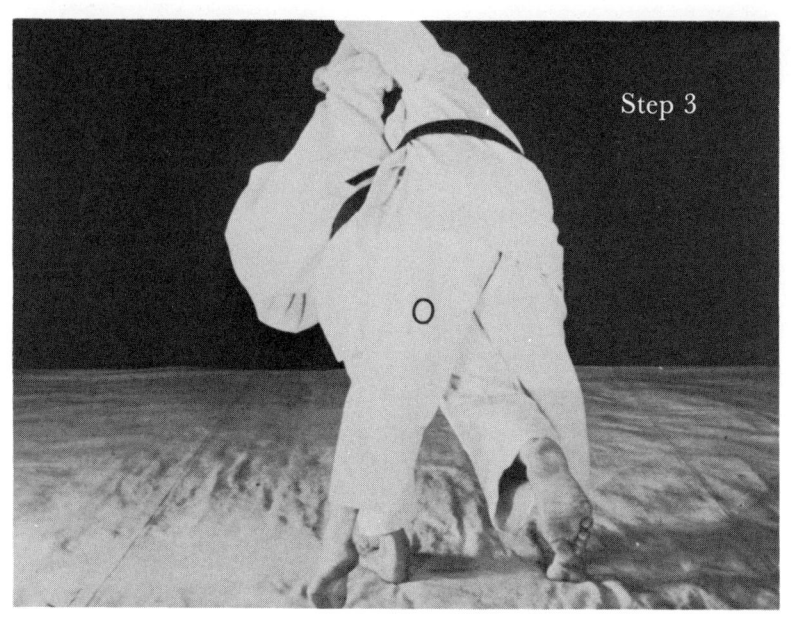

Step 3

Now reap his left inner thigh with the back of your right thigh (Step 3). With a simultaneous wheeling action of your hands, toss him over your loin (Step 4).

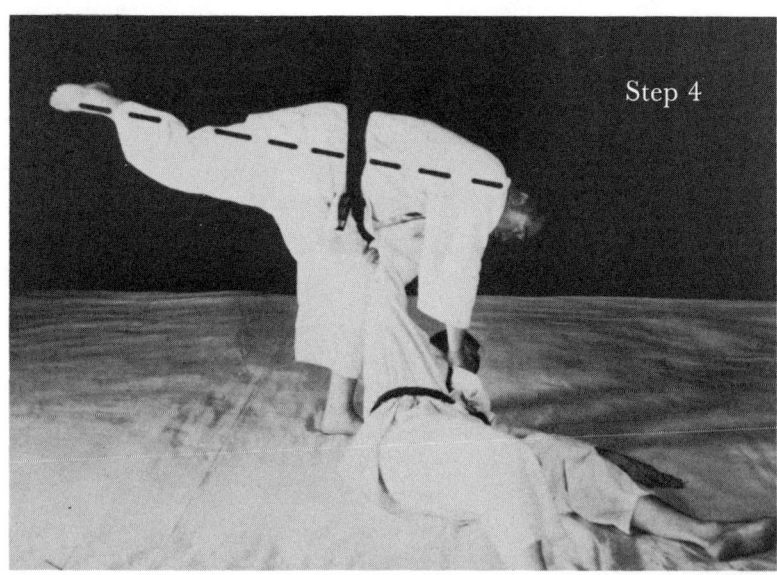

Step 4

TANDOKU-RENSHU

In the same way that a boxer shadow-boxes to improve his footwork and timing, a Judo player practices throwing without a partner. It's called Tandoku-Renshu, self-practice. Here we see the self-practice movements for Marote Seinage, the shoulder throw.

From an imaginary grasping of an opponent in the right natural posture, advance your right leg, knee bent, to the spot where your opponent's right foot would be. Then, pulling with your left hand and lifting with your right, pivot on the sole of your right foot—making a 180-degree turn (Steps 1 and 2).

Step 1

Step 2

Step 3

Step 4

Bring your left foot back parallel to your right foot with both knees bent (Step 3). At this precise moment suddenly straighten your knees, come up on your toes, bend your upper body forward and bring your hands and arms down in a pantomime of an actual throw (Step 4). The whole movement should be free flowing and continuous. You repeat this practice, changing to the left natural posture. Similar self-practice exercises can be used to perfect all of the Judo techniques.

This concludes the demonstration of throwing techniques. These beginning throws were selected from each of the many throwing methods existing. They are the introductory throws recommended by the Kodokan school in Tokyo. We confined ourselves solely to illustrating the various throws from the right natural posture, because after you have mastered the throws from the right side you will experience no great difficulty in applying the same methods to a left-hand start. Work hard to refine your throwing techniques—they will serve you well in your Judo days to come.

A quick throw

5. Mat Techniques

Step 1

In order to be a complete Judoka, you must learn how to handle yourself well on the mat. Judo experts say, "40 per cent of a player's training time should be devoted to the refinement of mat techniques." This is a study of these techniques, which are holds and escapes. The first technique we will demonstrate is Kesa-Gatame (scarf hold or lock). Approach your opponent by dropping to one knee, close to his chest, as shown in Step 1.

Then grasp his right arm at the elbow, drawing his arm deeply under your left armpit, as Step 2 illustrates from the side and the front. This gives you strong control of your opponent's right arm.

Now slide your right hand around his neck, and with your

right hand grasp the back of his collar with your thumb inside. With your entire right side pressing tightly against his chest, keep your right leg bent and your thigh tight against his arm and shoulder. Extend your left leg behind you to create a firm base (Step 3). Keeping your chin in, lower your head until it

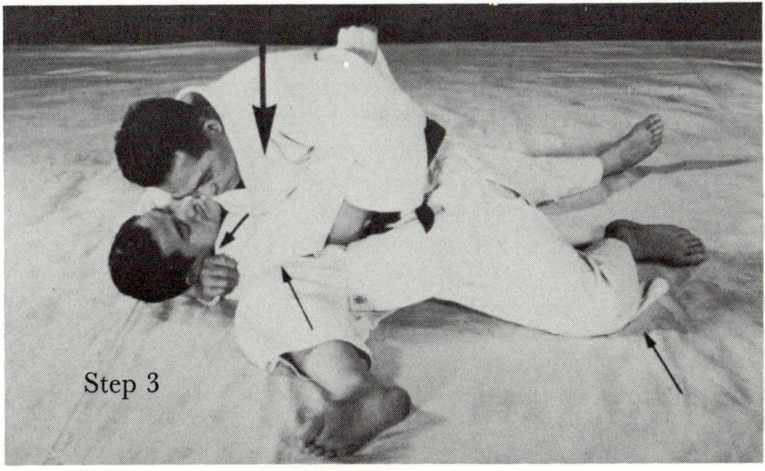

Step 1

touches your opponent's cheek and hold him down, thus gaining complete control of the upper quarter of his body.

For every holding action in Judo there are one or more escape techniques. This is one of the most common escapes from the scarf hold you have just seen. Reach around and grasp the holder's belt with both hands, and at the same time bring your heels close to the rear of your own hips (Step 1).

Bring yourself up on your head and toes (Step 2 shows front and rear views). By twisting your body to your left you will lift and turn him in a large circle, rolling him over your body.

Another escape from the scarf hold begins the same way. Grasp your foe's belt with both hands and at the same time bring your heels in close to your hips, as you did in the first escape. Next, start to bring yourself up by bridging—creating space between yourself and the mat. Quickly twisting your body clockwise, free your right arm and wriggle out on your knees and stomach (Steps 1 and 2).

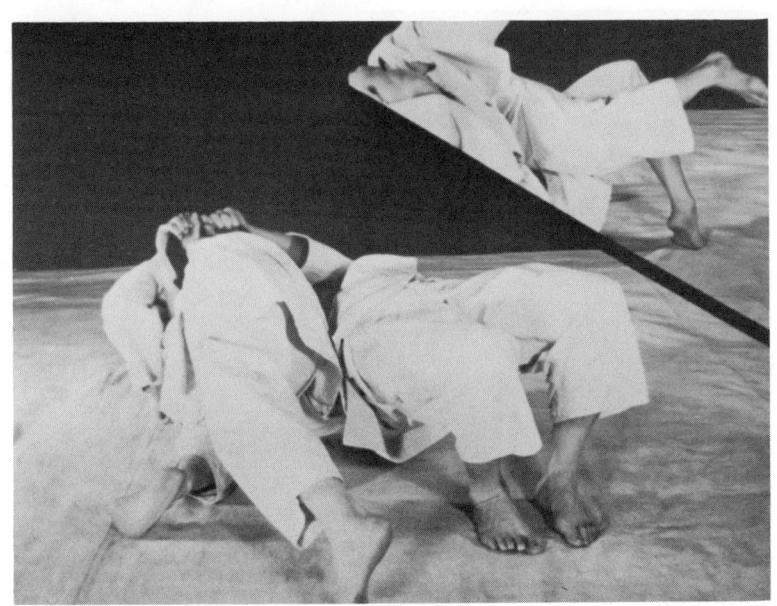

Step 2

Steps 1 and 2

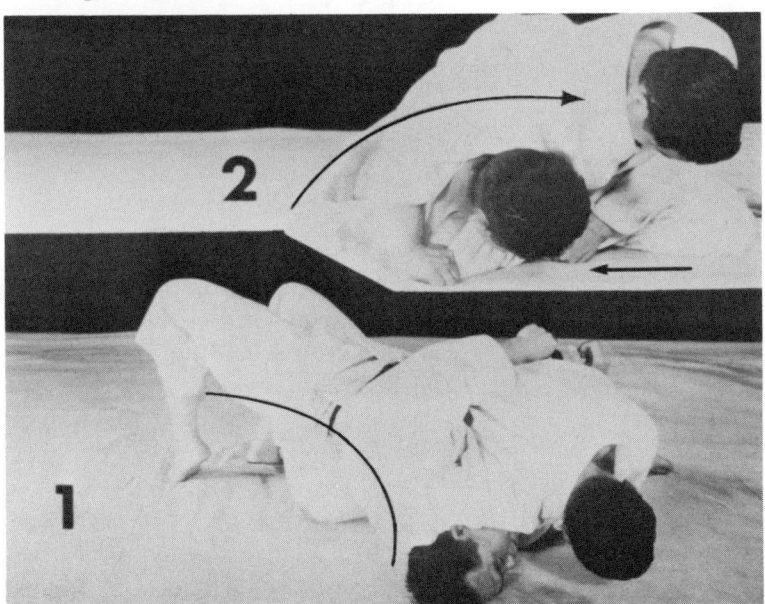

In a third escape from the scarf hold, after you bring yourself up and twist your body to the right, free your right arm and shoulder from his grip. Force your right knee underneath your competitor's body (Step 1).

Step 1

Immediately wrap his left leg with both of your legs (Step 2).

Step 2

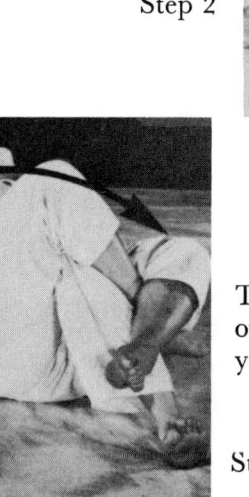

Twisting to the left, turn him over on his left side, freeing yourself (Step 3).

Step 3

One of the best opportunities to escape from Kesa-Gatame occurs at the very beginning of the hold. Before your opponent can completely control your right shoulder—quickly grab his right arm by the elbow with your left hand and slip it past your head. This enables you to turn clockwise to your stomach to escape.

 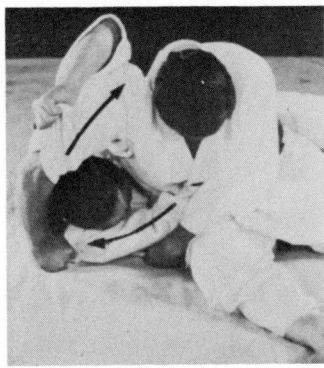

Grab his elbow *Turn clockwise*

Kuzure-Kesa-Gatame is the modified scarf hold. Hold your opponent's right arm firmly under your left armpit. The upper side of his body is held under the right side of your chest, and your right leg is held tight against his body. Your left leg is

extended back and bent at the knee. Lower your head until it presses against his cheek, holding him down.

To escape this hold when it is being applied to you, transfer your body position to the far left of your opponent, then raise both legs high in the direction of his head. At the same time, place your left arm in front of his neck (Step 1).

Then bring your legs quickly downward with a snap so the force of their momentum carries your head and shoulders upward, half-reversing positions with your opponent (Steps 2 and 3).

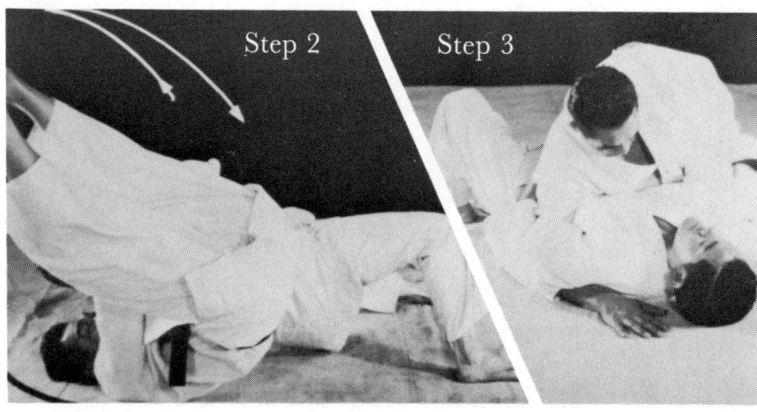

Step 1

Step 2

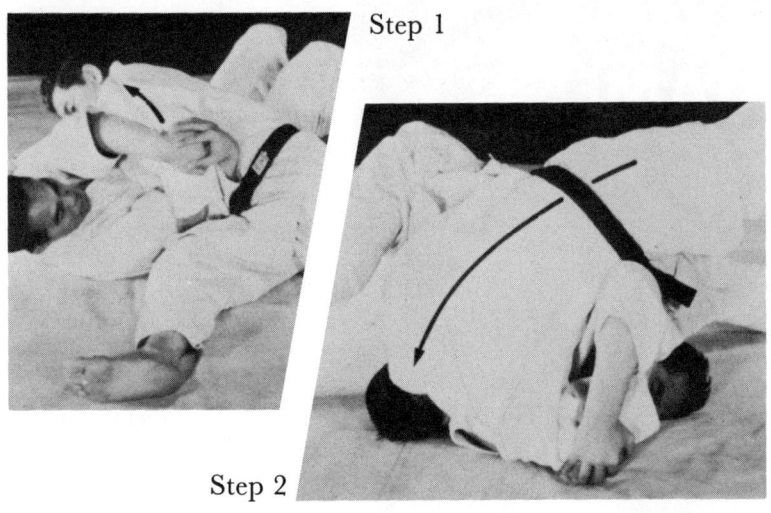

An alternative way to escape from this hold is to pull your right arm close to your side. Then reach across with your left hand, locking both hands around his elbow, as shown in Step 1. Pull him up by twisting your body in the direction of his left shoulder, and turn him over (Step 2). Hold him down, as shown in Step 3.

Step 3

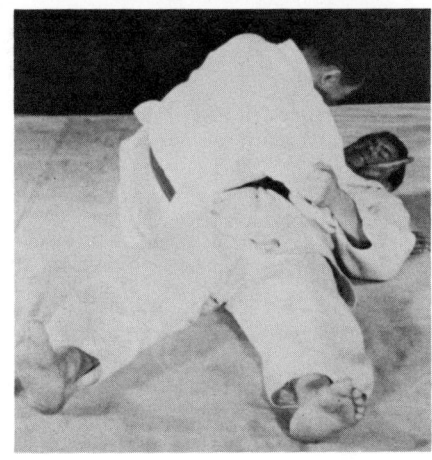

The next mat technique is Kata-Gatame, the shoulder lock. As illustrated in Step 1, approach your opponent from his right side. Grasping his right arm with both of yours, raise it and press it against his right cheek (Step 2).

Step 1

Step 2

Step 3

Pass your right arm over the tip of his left shoulder and under his neck. With the right side of your neck and shoulder controlling his right arm, pass your left arm over the tip of his left shoulder, and under his neck until both of your hands meet and clasp (Step 3).

From this position, advance your bent, right knee until the knee presses against his right side. Your toes are down and your left leg is extended straight out to your left side to form a rigid triangle (Step 4).

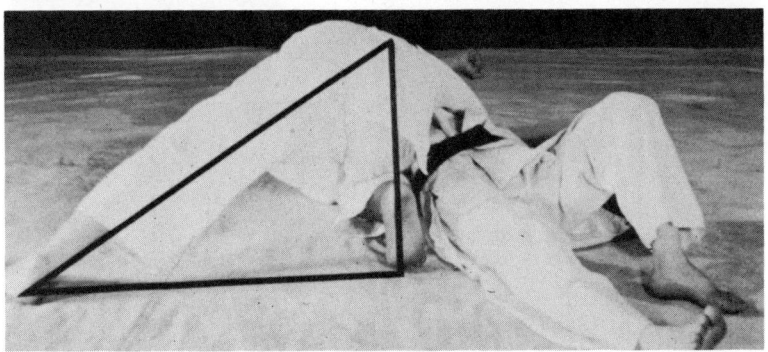

Step 4

Reverse positions and place yourself in the role of the person being held. Here is an escape from the shoulder lock. First,

Step 1

bring your heels close to your hips and bridge upward. At the same time, twist your body to the right to pull your trapped right arm partially out. Then clasp your hands together and push him away to create space (Step 1). Quickly bring your legs over in a somersault and pull your arm out (Step 2).

Step 2

An alternative method of escaping is, after you bridge, to grab his belt with both hands and suddenly twist your body to the left, rolling him over.

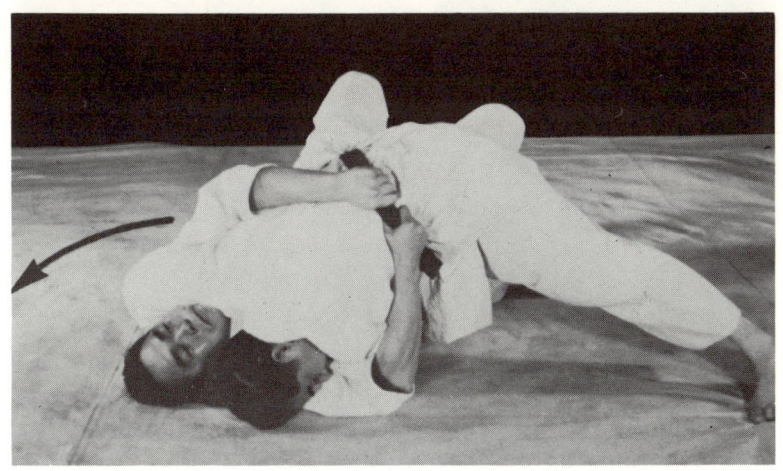

An alternate escape

In Kami-Shiho-Gatame, the locking of the upper four quarters, approach your opponent from his head. Then bring your knees up snug to your opponent's shoulders, as shown in Step 1.

Step 1

KAMI-SHIHO-GATAME

Passing both hands beneath his arms, grasp both sides of his belt with your thumbs turned upward. Turn your head sideways and press it against his stomach (Step 2). Lower your loins so your stomach presses down on his head. Hold him down like this, pinning him from four directions (Step 3).

When the position is reversed and you find yourself in the plight of being held, here is one of the common escapes from the upper-four-quarters lock. Push your opponent upwards by bridging. Then, putting both hands on his upper lapel, push upwards. While your arms are still extended, suddenly lower your body and round your shoulders and back. Bring both knees under his shoulders. By pushing him upward, you will escape to the side.

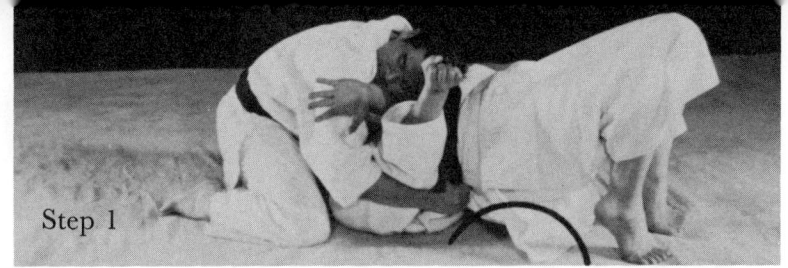

Step 1

In another escape from the same hold, bring both of your feet close to your hips and raise your body upwards. Place your left hand under your opponent's neck, creating space between your back and the mat (Step 1). As you lower your body, twist

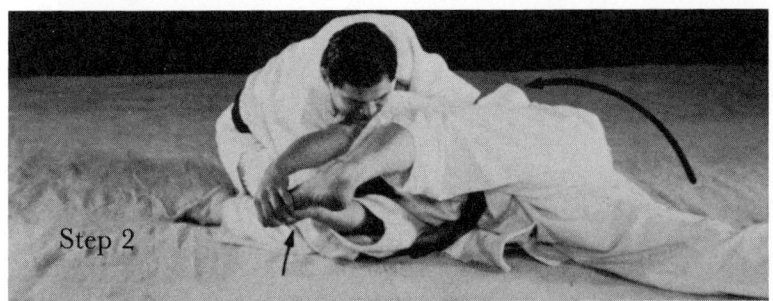

Step 2

your hip to the right side, swinging your left leg over you. Grasp it with both hands (Step 2). Push the holder away with the combined force of your arms and leg, and at the same time, effect your escape by first rolling your body to your right, then quickly in the opposite direction, sliding out on your left side (Step 3).

Step 3

Step 1

Kuzure-Kami-Shiho-Gatame is the modified locking of the upper four quarters. As your opponent lies on his back, approach and take a position between his right shoulder and head (Step 1).

Bringing both knees in close to his body, slip your right arm under his armpit and grasp the back of his collar, with your four fingers inside and thumb outside (Step 2).

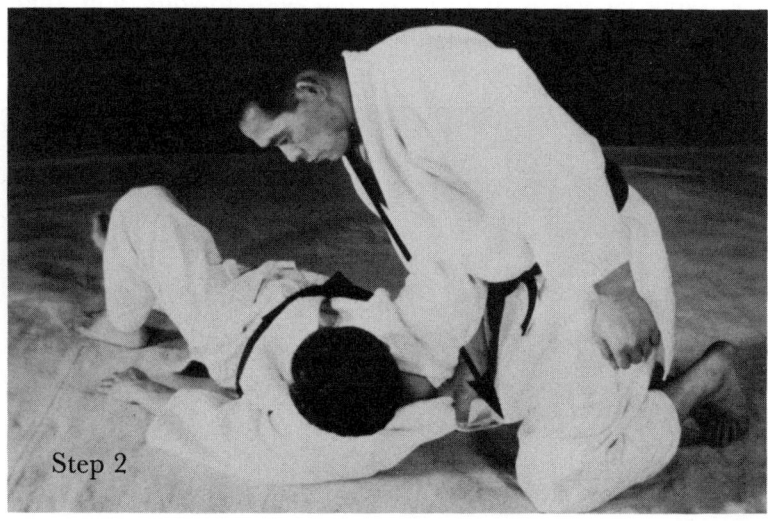

Step 2

Step 3

Pass your left hand under his left shoulder, and grasp the back of his belt with your left hand—thumb inside (Step 3).

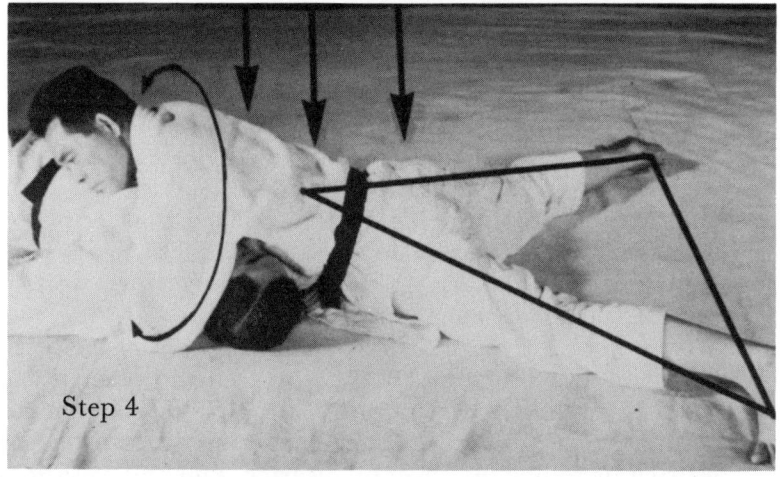

Step 4

Close both your arms, straighten your upper body and hold him with your feet spread-eagled to exert counter-pressure in any direction of resistance (Step 4). If the situation warrants, you may also grasp his belt with both hands.

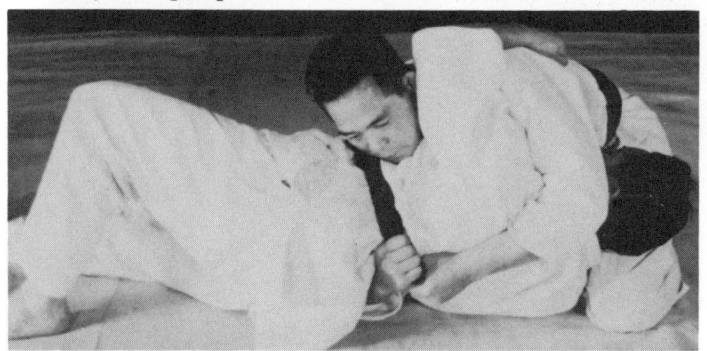

Grasp belt with two hands

Step 1

Since Kuzure-Kami-Shiho is a widely used Judo-holding technique, escape knowledge is essential. First, reach over his right shoulder and grab his belt with your left hand. Then apply a series of bridging and bucking actions. After each successive bridge, twist your body to the right—finally pulling your trapped right arm loose! At the same time, work your body up perpendicular to his (Step 1).

After your right arm is free, grasp the front of his belt and push him away, floating his body upward with your left hand (Step 2). As your opponent pushes forward to reconsolidate his position, slide your right knee under his stomach and free yourself by rolling him over on his back. Pull and push in with your hands (Step 3).

Step 2

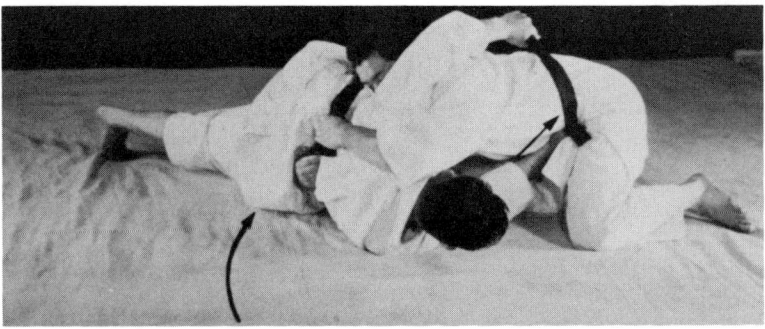

Step 3

Step 1

In Yoko-Shiho-Gatame—the side-four-quarter hold—approach the side of your opponent (Step 1).

Step 2

Using both hands, raise your opponent's right arm and place it parallel to your left side (Step 2).

Next, pass your right arm under his left thigh and grasp his belt with your hands—thumb inside—drawing him in (Step 3).

Continuing your hold, slip your left arm under his neck grasping the lapel near his left shoulder with your left hand, encircling his whole body with your arms. With your head

Step 3

against his chest, apply even pressure over the entire body area, rendering him immobile (Step 4).

Then draw both legs up as seen here from the rear in Step 5. Your right kneecap presses against his right loin and your left kneecap is pushed up snugly under his right armpit, rendering his right arm and leg useless.

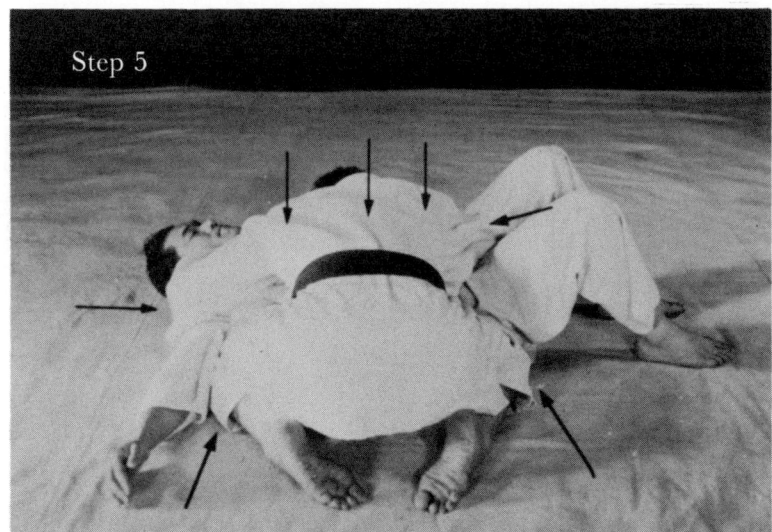

Or you may hold him in this position, with the freedom to extend either leg to counter-escape maneuvers.

When locked in the side-four-quarter hold there are several escape methods you may use. However, you must execute some preliminary maneuvers to create "working room." First, place your left hand on your opponent's collar and grasp his belt near his left hip. Then press down and away with both hands, moving him towards your thigh and sliding upward at the same time (Step 1).

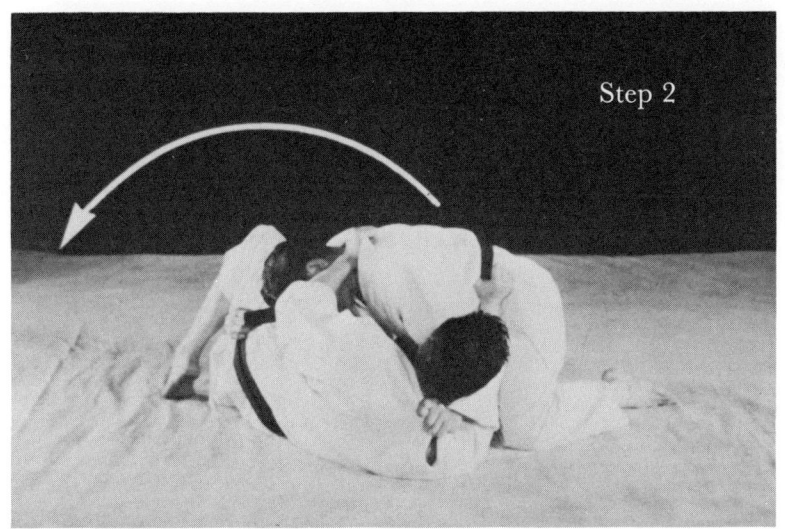

Step 2

Then bridge your body upward and lower your body on your right side, still holding your opponent away. Keep repeating this movement until there is sufficient room to place your right knee under his and roll him over (Step 2).

Or you can bring your right arm under his chest and quickly reverse your direction by twisting to the left to free your right arm from under his left armpit.

Twisting to the left

Triangle escape

Another way to escape is to push your opponent down far enough to swing your left leg over his head behind his neck. Apply a scissor with your right knee-pit, forming a triangle to control his head, shoulders and arm.

One of the most popular grappling techniques is Kuzure-Yoko-Shiho, the modified lateral locking of four quarters. This pinning principle closely follows Yoko-Shiho, shown previously. The only distinct modification is that the left hand is extended over your opponent's left shoulder, keeping his left arm immobile by locking it securely between your back and left shoulder. Continuing from here, keep your body low, applying even pressure on his chest (Step 1). Then reach under his left

Step 1

Step 2

leg with your right hand and grasp the seat of his pants, as shown in Step 2, locking him in from four directions. The position of your legs follows the same pattern as in regular Yoko-Shiho.

Step 1

Here is a widely used escape method from this hold. Bridge upward with your body, then quickly slide away from him by twisting to your right. At the same time, your right hand pushes against his left hip and your left forearm pushes his head down toward your belt (Step 1).

Step 2

Passing both your hands down through the open space underneath his chest, grab your right foot and push his body upward, stretching your right leg at the same time (Step 2). Complete rolling to the right on your stomach and break his hold.

In Tate-Shiho-Gatame, the lengthwise locking of the four quarters, drop to your left knee to the right side of your

Step 1

TATE-SHIHO-GATAME

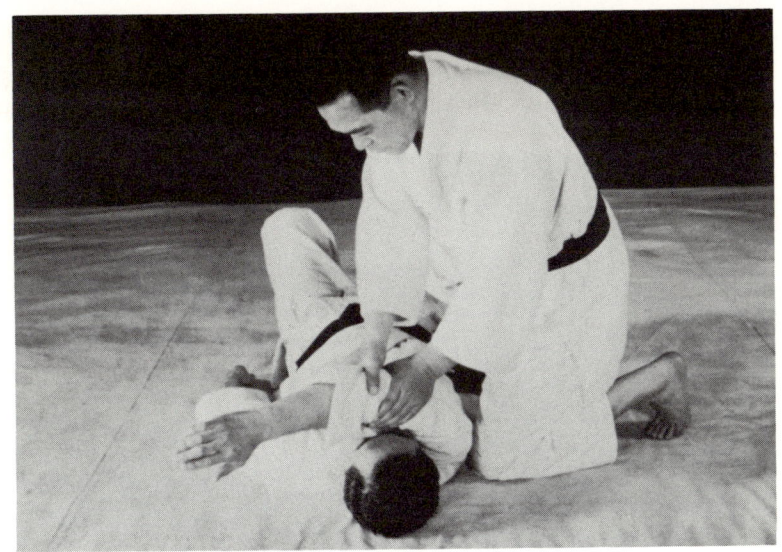

Step 2

opponent (Step 1). Then grasp his right arm with both hands and press it down against his cheek (Step 2).

Step 3

Release your right hand and grasp his left arm, pushing it outward. At the same time straddle his body (Step 3).

Then slide your right arm over his left shoulder and clasp your left hand as shown in Step 4, completely tying up his right arm and shoulder. Bend forward so your neck and right arm

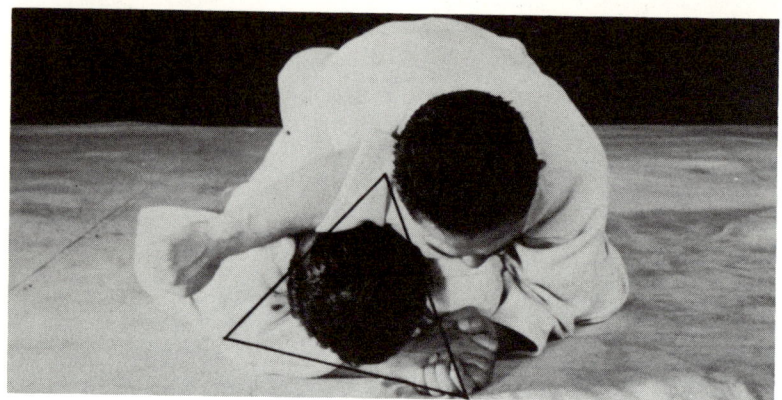

Step 4

form a triangle. Now bring your head down and hold your opponent with the full weight of your body (Step 5).

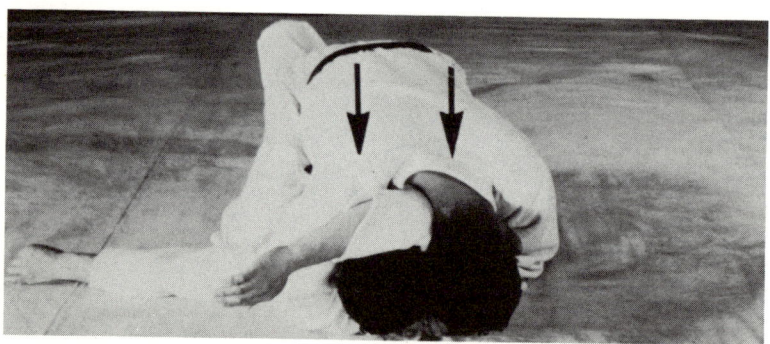

Step 5

Completed hold

Here is a dramatic view of the completed hold from a rear perspective. Note the position of the feet controlling his hips—an action not visible in the other scenes.

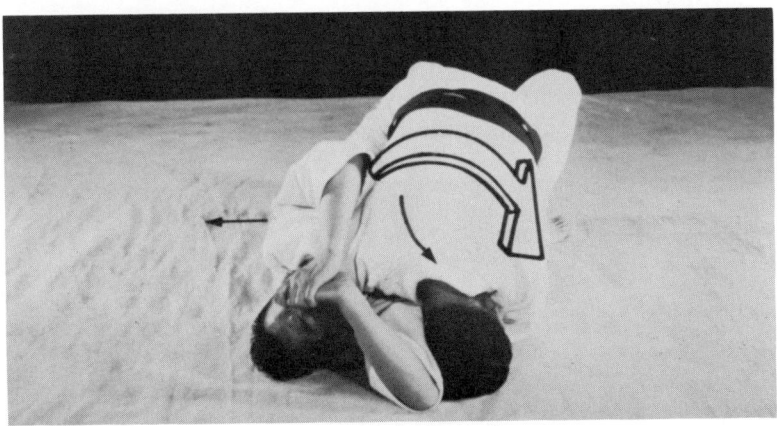

Standard escape

For a standard escape, from the bottom position clasp both hands and force his head downward, breaking his hold on your right shoulder. Then roll to the right to escape.

Step 1

In another escape, grab your opponent's right pant leg at the ankle and pull his leg up, shifting his weight well forward (Step 1).

Then wrap both of your legs around his right leg and turn him over, either to the right or the left, and effect your escape (Step 2).

A point to remember is that you are not a completely trained Judoka until you perfect the mat techniques too. The ability to handle yourself when the action is taken to the mat is an essential part of the mastering of Judo.

Step 2

6. Offensive and Defensive Mat Techniques

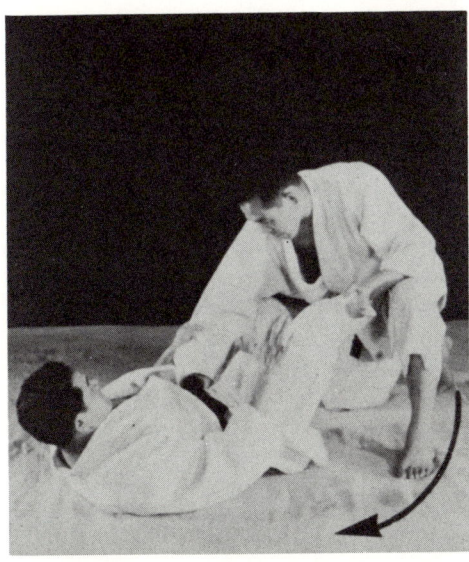

Opponent's defensive position

Offensive mat approaches come into Judo most often as a follow-up after a throw. It is not very difficult to follow up if the opponent is unprepared to take a defensive mat position after he is thrown. However, if he quickly recovers from the throw and takes the proper defensive position—by placing his legs towards you—it is very difficult to continue your attack, unless you know your offensive mat techniques.

The primary obstacle in securing a good pinning hold is penetrating your opponent's defense. To break through his guard and successfully apply your grappling technique, it's

Breaking through opponent's defense

usually necessary to begin with some preliminary maneuvering designed to gain a position for a good pinning hold.

Here is a proper offensive mat posture, as refined by the Kodokan. Your center of gravity is low, yet at the same time you have freedom of mobility in all directions. Your knees are bent, hips down, with your toes on the mat to provide quick change in any direction. For an example of how you continue your offense from this posture, move in and cradle both of his

Offensive mat position

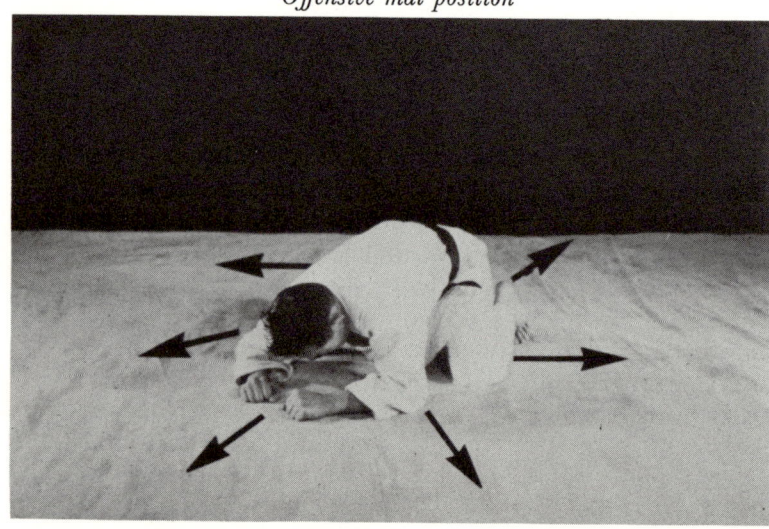

legs firmly in your arms. Then, keeping your body low and your feet wide apart, push him forward (Step 1).

As he pushes back, suddenly pull back and drop his legs between your legs. Then slide quickly upwards and hold his upper body stationary (Step 2).

Step 3

Now pivot to your left, and attack his right flank by bringing your left knee against his right arm, securing the side locking of the four quarters (Step 3).

In an attack immediately after a throw, come down to a posture on one knee, grasping his belt with one hand to hold him in position. Then, grasping his pant leg with the other hand, hold his leg where it is while you move around and attack his right flank.

An attack after a throw

Pulling opponent up

In another method, pull your opponent up on his rear haunches and then go in on either side or over his lowered legs.

Still another mat approach is to grasp his pant leg and sleeve, pull him aside and attack his flank. Or move around to attack from his head.

Pulling him to you

In a situation where your opponent has been thrown and you remain standing, you may continue your offensive by grasping both of his ankles and sweeping his legs first to his right then back to his left, moving his legs from your approach path (Step 1).

Then quickly step in on his right side, pinning his right hip with your right knee (Step 2) and conclude the hold by pro-

ceeding to apply Kesa-Gatame or Kata-Gatame. Or, by grasping both pants legs at the knees, press down and to his left (Step 1).

Entering from his right side, immobilize his body with your right knee as you proceed to a pinning technique (Step 2).

Grasping opponent's belt

Another way to break through your opponent's defensive posture is to grasp his belt. With your right hand and knee, press down against his inner thigh. Then slide up on his side for a pin hold.

In the shoulder method of approach, split your opponent's legs. Control his right leg by encircling it with your left arm, and then lock it tightly with your arm, shoulder and neck. Press your left shoulder forward towards his chest and at the same time hold his left leg down, with your right hand grasping his trousers (Step 1).

Step 1

Step 2

Then bring your right knee over his left thigh so that your shin presses his thigh down tight to the mat. Now, moving your right hand up from his leg, grasp his left sleeve near the elbow and pull upward to clear his left side for your pin (Step 2).

In an alternative to the previous approach, after lifting his right leg with your shoulder, split his legs as before. Quickly move your left knee up against his haunch in a wedging action (Step 1).

Step 1

Step 2

Now, while your shoulder and your right hand are forcing your opponent to roll slightly to the right, quickly turn your body to the left and pivot your shoulder on his leg, swinging your right leg in a wide arc (Step 2).

After turning more than 90 degrees to the right you will end up in the position shown in Step 3, securing him with Kuzure-Yoko-Shiho—the modified side four-corner pin.

Step 3

Another way of getting past your opponent's leg defense is the pull-up technique. After grabbing both of your opponent's legs at the knees pull your arms inward and upward (Step 1).

Step 1

Move in close enough to grasp his belt on the left and right side of his torso. With this better leverage continue your pushing action, rolling him back until his legs harmlessly paw the air and his shoulders are on the mat (Step 2).

Step 2

Step 3

Sweep around to his right side. Pin his right arm with your left leg as shown in Step 3, applying your pin from the side.

Many times—especially during your beginning Judo training, when you'll be wrestling other inexperienced players—your opponent may take defensive action by lying on his stomach. When this occurs quickly move to his side, your body forming a "T" with this position. Slip one hand under his chin and grab his lapel very deep. Slide the other hand underneath his chest, reaching across to grasp his far arm near his elbow. Then place your shoulder against his body and push, at the same time pulling with both hands. Driving with your legs wide apart roll him over on his back. He is then open for Yoko-Shiho-Gatame, the side-locking of the four quarters.

The "T" position

Step 1

In Step 1 is the beginning of a "head on" approach moving to a sideward twisting technique. Grab his belt at the back with your right hand. Hook your left arm under his right armpit, anchoring that hand by grasping your right lapel. Now, twist your opponent to the right. Slide yourself to the left, and with the combined pushing action of your shoulder and pulling motion of your right hand, roll him over on his back (Step 2) and right into Kuzure-Yoko-Shiho, the modified side-locking of the four quarters.

Step 2

KUZURE-YOKO-SHIHO

When applying this offensive technique, if you encounter particularly stiff resistance to your upward twist (Step 1) you can accomplish your objective in another way. Capitalizing on his resistance, quickly reverse direction downward, rolling to your left in a counter-clockwise movement (Step 2). He will

Step 1

Step 2

roll completely over on his back (Step 3), where you can follow up with Kami-Shiho-Gatame. If your opponent attempts to

Step 3

KAMI-SHIHO-GATAME

resist your twisting efforts by moving upward, slide your right foot forward between his legs (Step 1). Lean back, as shown in Step 2.

Step 1

With your right leg against his left inner thigh (Step 3) flip him directly backwards over your right shoulder (Step 4).

Step 4

You can end on top, and apply Tate-Shiho-Gatame.

Whenever you find yourself on the mat, either thrown by your opponent or missing a throw and falling, immediately face

TATE-SHIHO-GATAME

Step 1

your opponent in the defensive posture shown in Step 1. If your opponent moves to either side, move with him with your legs serving as a barrier against his attack.

As he makes his offensive approach, place your right foot on his left hip (Step 2). At the same time, place your left leg outside of his body, your foot on his right inner thigh. Place your right hand on his left inner lapel and your left hand on his elbow.

Step 2

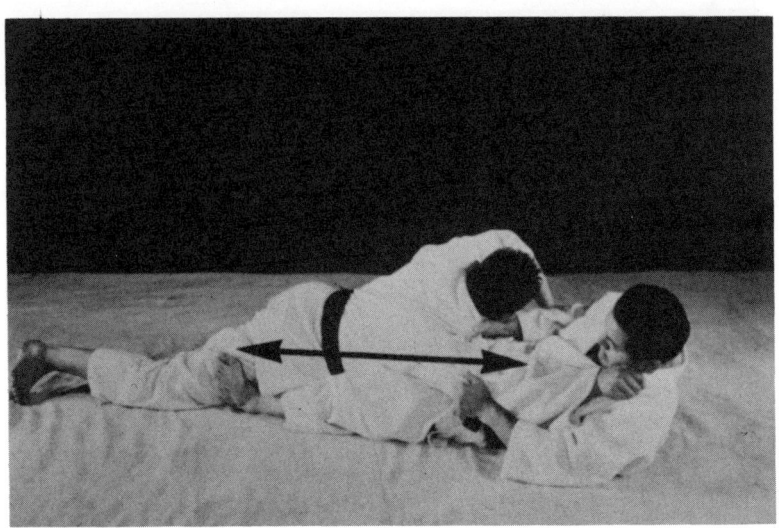

Step 3

Then, by pushing with your feet and pulling with your hands you will stretch him flat on his stomach and stop his forward movement (Step 3).

As he moves forward again, hook your left leg over his right leg as shown in Step 4, and at the same time lock his right forearm against your chest. Now shift your right foot under his

Step 5

left leg and flip him over to the side on his back (Step 5). Then roll over on top to apply Tate-Shiho-Gatame.

For a variation of the previous technique, reach over and grasp his belt with your right hand. His right arm is secured with your left hand. Anchor your arm by holding your own right lapel (Step 1).

Step 1

Step 2

Your feet are deployed in the same manner as the previous sequence to provide you with a pinning advantage (Step 2).

If your opponent breaks through your defense, you must stop him immediately from making any further progress. This is, accomplished by wrapping your legs around one of his legs as you see in Step 3. Then proceed to free the parts of your body which are confined.

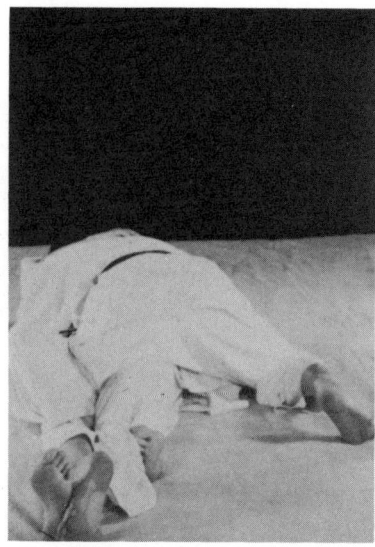

Step 3

A good defense from the opponent's sideward approach is the use of the body bind. When your opponent moves around to your side, roll to your side (Step 1).

Step 1

Lock his encircling arm tightly under your armpit, binding his body to you, and roll to the left (Step 2).

Step 2

Step 3

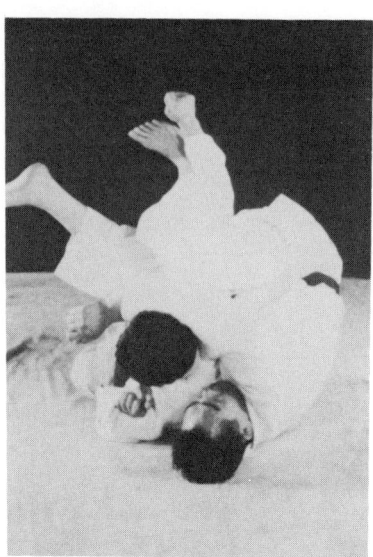

Step 4

Carry him over your back, placing yourself in a favorable position to apply a pin (Steps 3 and 4).

TOMOE-NAGE

Tomoe-Nage, the circle throw, is part of a series of Judo methods known as the sacrifice throws—so-called because you sacrifice your relatively safe standing position, and throw your opponent by going to the mat yourself.

Starting from the right natural posture, push him back as though to break his balance to the rear (Step 1).

As he pushes back to regain his balance, quickly change your left hand from the sleeve to his right lapel and *pull* him well forward and upward on his toes. At the same time, bend your right knee deeply to lower your body and slide your left foot well between his legs (Step 2).

Step 1

Step 2

"O" identifies opponent

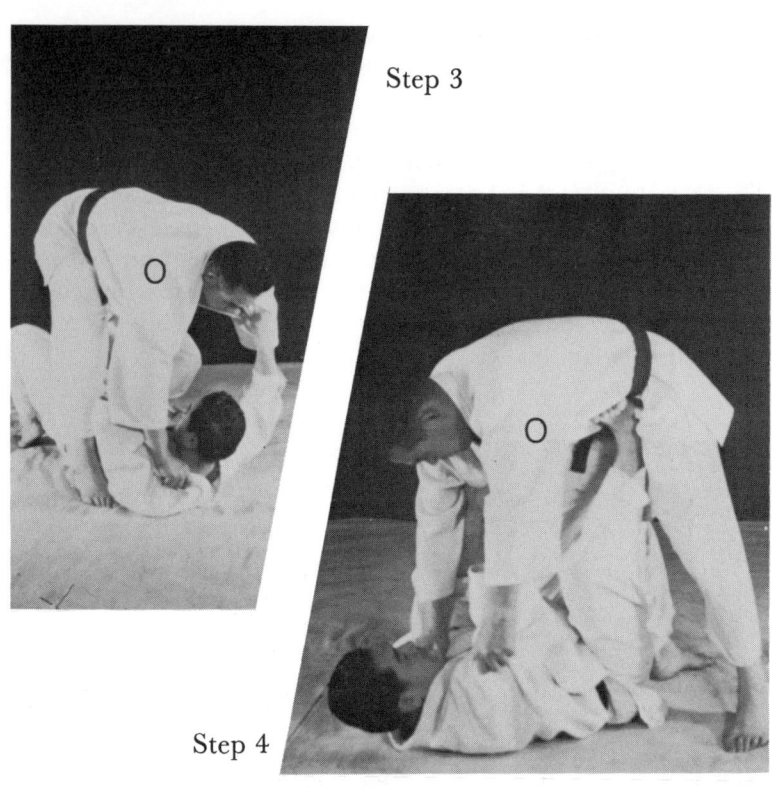

Step 3

Step 4

Roll backwards and slide your body underneath him while continuing to pull in a wide arc with both hands (Step 3). Bring your right foot up so that the sole meets his lower abdomen in the middle of his forward arc. NOTE: It is important that you pull your opponent on to your foot just as he reaches 12 o'clock in his forward circle (Step 4).

O = Opponent

Straightening your knee to provide additional propulsion, add to his toppling momentum by throwing your arms directly backwards with a slight upward pull at the end (Step 5).

Step 5

He will somersault over you and on to the mat in a straight line with your body, as shown in Step 6.

Step 6

SEIRI-UNDO

The purpose of Seiri-Undo or restoration exercise is to bring the body back to normal condition after a strenuous workout. About 2 or 3 minutes is sufficient.

Beginning the exercises

First, lie flat on your stomach in a relaxed manner and have your partner gently pull forward and upward to stretch the muscles.

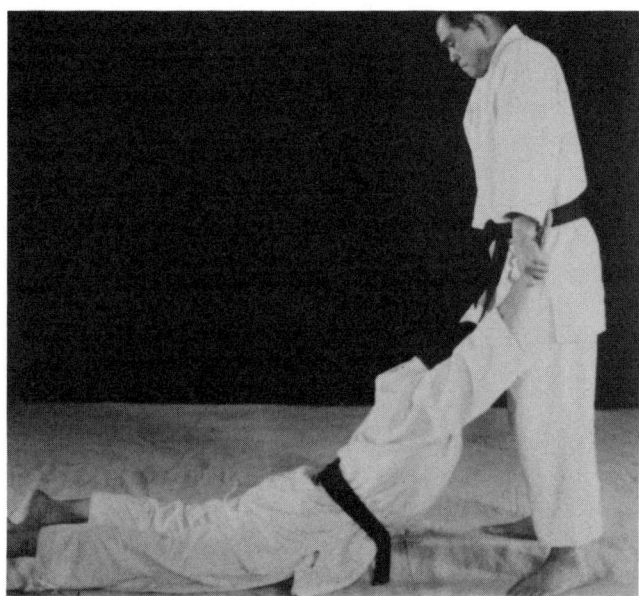

Stretching stomach muscles

An alternative method is to straddle your partner, gently lift his upper body by grasping his wrists. Raise and lower him several times.

Straddling your partner

Another method is the back-to-back stretching. When being lifted, remain completely relaxed.

Stretching back-to-back

In the deep-breathing exercises, inhale deeply and slowly as you bring your hands upward. Then exhale slowly as your hands are brought down to your sides.

About to exhale

Now you are probably wondering how to win a Judo match. There are three ways to win.

A forceful throw

You can throw your opponent to the mat with such force and skill that you are awarded an "Ippon" or full point by the referee. Such a throw would end the match and you would be awarded the victory.

If your throw is not perfect, you are given a "Waza-Ari" or half a point. The match continues until you earn another half point. If the time limit runs out before either opponent earns a full point, the Judoka holding a Waza-Ari is declared the winner.

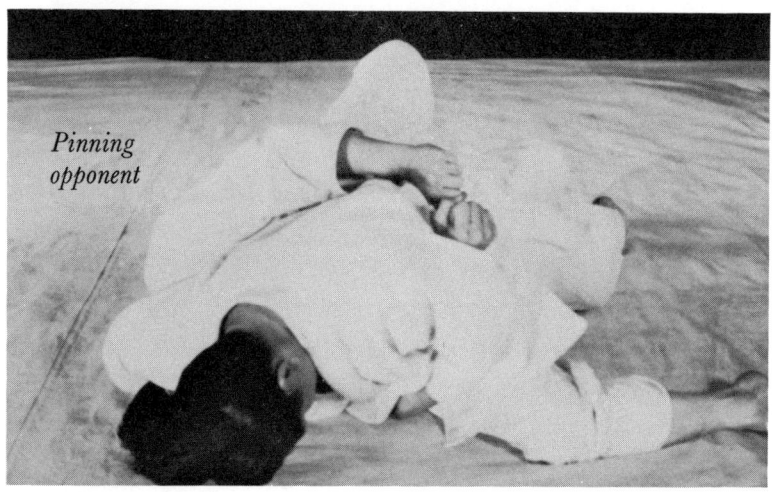

Pinning opponent

A second way of winning is by a pin. A Judo pin is different from a wrestling pin, since in Judo you do *not* have to hold your opponent's shoulders to the mat. You win by simply controlling your opponent's body with one of the Judo holds for 30 seconds. If you already hold a half point, you need only control him for 25 seconds.

Finally, you can be awarded the match by applying one of the Judo choking holds to your opponent until he concedes.

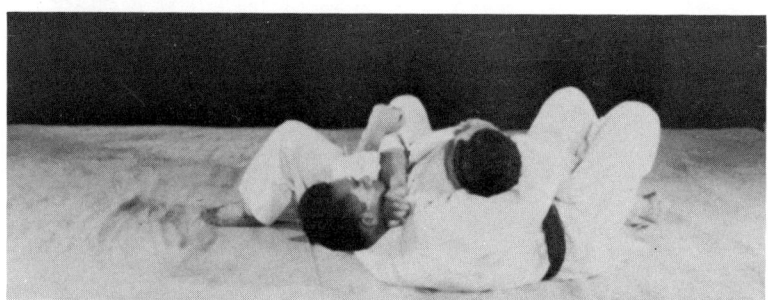

A Judo choking hold

A throw

A hold

This ends our introduction to Judo. Judo, like any other sport, requires practice and conditioning to achieve the most from your talents. Remember, Judo is more than just a contact sport—it's a physical culture and a philosophy as well. So work hard and practice well. You'll be pleased with the personal rewards you'll gain from Judo, the gentle art.

Moving on the offense

Index

Approaches on mat, offensive, 126–142
Ashi-Waza (throw with foot and leg), 50 ff.
   De-Ashi-Harai (advancing foot sweep), 52–53
   Harai-Goshi (sweeping loin throw), 88–90
   Hiza-Guruma (knee wheel), 54–57
   Ko-Soto-Gari (minor outside reap), 74–76
   Ko-Uchi-Gari (minor inside reap), 76–77
   Okuri-Ashi-Harai (sweeping ankle throw), 83–85
   O-Soto-Gari (major outer reap), 62–64
   O-Uchi-Gari (major inner reap), 67–68
   Sasai-Tsurikomi-Ashi (propping-drawing-ankle throw), 64–66
   Uchi-Mata (inner thigh throw), 90–92
Backfalls, 36–39, from sitting, 36–37, from standing, 39, from squat, 37–38
Back snake crawl, 23
Basic stances, 24–26
   Hidari-Shizentai, 25, 26
   Hon-Shizentai, 24, 26
   Migi-Shizentai, 25, 26
Basic grip, 26–27
   from left stance, 27
Bending to side, 16–17
Body bridge, 22
Breakfalls, 24–48
   basic stance, grip, 24–27
   Kuzushi (upsetting opponent's balance), 30–32
   moving forward and sideways, 28–29
   Tai-Sabaki (turns), 29–30
   Ukemi (breaking fall) exercises, 32–48
Ceremony, Judo, 10–14
Colors of belts, ranks, 14
De-Ashi-Harai (advancing foot sweep), 52–53
Diving somersaults, 46
Escape techniques, 98–124
Forward falls, 47–48
Forward somersault, 42–45
Harai-Goshi (sweeping loin throw), 88–90
Hidari-Shizentai (stance, left foot forward), 25, 26
History, 5–6
   Kodokan school, 6
   originator of sport, 5–6
Hiza-Guruma (knee wheel), 54–57
Hon-Shizentai (stance, feet parallel), 24, 26
Ippon (full point award), 154–155
Ippon-Seoi-Nage (one-hand-over-the-shoulder throw), 69–70
Judo ceremony, 10–14
Judogi (Judo uniform), 7–9, 14
Judoka (Judo players), ranks, 14

Kami-Shiho-Gatami (locking of the upper four quarters), 107–109
  escapes from, 108–109
Kano, Jigaro, originator of sport, 5–6
Kata-Gatame (shoulder lock), 104–106
  escapes from, 105–106
Kesa-Gatame (scarf hold or lock), 96–101
  escapes from, 98–101
Kochi-Waza (hip techniques, throwing), 58 ff.
  O-Goshi (major loin throw), 60–61
  Sodi-Tsuri-Komi-Goshi (sleeve-lifting-pull-hip throw), 81–82
  Tsuri-Komi-Goshi (lift-pull-hip-throw), 78–80
  Uki-Goshi (floating hip throw), 58–59
Ko-Soto-Gari (minor outside reap with foot), 74–76
Ko-Uchi-Gari (minor inside reap with foot), 76–77
Kuzure-Kami-Shiho-Gatame (modified locking of the upper four quarters), 110–113
  escapes from, 112–113
Kuzure-Kesa-Gatame (modified scarf hold), 101–103
  escapes from, 102–103
Kuzure-Yoko-Shiho (modified side-four-quarter hold), 118–120
  escapes from, 119–120
Kuzushi (upsetting opponent's balance), 30–32
Loosening ankles, 18, knees, 17, neck, 16
Marote-Seoi-Nage (two-arm-shoulder throw), 71–73
  self-practice, 93–95
Match, 154–157
  choking hold, 156–157
  Ippon (full-point award), 154–155
  pin, 156
  Waza-Ari (half-point award), 156
Mat techniques, 96–151
  Kami-Shiho-Gatame (locking of the upper four quarters), 107–109
  Kata-Gatame (shoulder lock), 104–106
  Kesa-Gatame (scarf hold or lock), 96–101
  Kuzure-Kami-Shiho-Gatame (modified locking of the upper four quarters), 110–113
  Kuzure-Kesa-Gatame (modified scarf hold), 101–103
  Kuzure-Yoko-Shiho (modified side-four-quarter hold), 118–120
  Offensive and defensive techniques, 125–151
  Tate-Shiho-Gatame (lengthwise locking of the four quarters), 120–124
  Yoko-Shiho-Gatame (side-four-quarter hold), 113–118
Migi-Shizentai (stance, right foot forward), 25, 26
Moving forward on mat, 28
  sideways, 29
Offensive and defensive mat techniques, 125–151
  approaches, offensive, 126–142
  positions, defensive, 142–148
  posture, offensive, 126
  Tomoe-Nage (circle throw), 149–151
O-Goshi (major loin throw), 60–61
Okuri-Ashi-Harai (sweeping ankle throw), 83–85
One-hand somersault, 45
O-Soto-Gari (major outer reap with foot), 62–64
O-Uchi-Gari (major inner reap with foot), 67–68
Positions, defensive, 142–148
Posture, offensive, 126
Push-ups, 19
Ranks, Judoka (Judo players), 14
Rei (referee's command), 10

Rocking on front and back, 20
Sasai-Tsurikomi-Ashi (propping-drawing-ankle throw), 64–66
Seiri-Undo (restoration exercise), 152–154
   back-to-back, 153
   deep breathing, 154
   on stomach, 152–153
Sidefalls, from sitting, 40, from standing, 42, from squatting, 41
Sodi-Tsuri-Komi-Goshi (sleeve-lifting-pull-hip throw), 81–82
Somersaults, 42–46, diving, 46, forward, 42–45, one-hand, 45
Stretching leg muscles, 18, 19, 20
Swinging and pivoting, 15
Tache-Re (standing bow), 10–11
Tachi-Waza (throw from standing), 49–95
   Ashi-Waza (leg and foot techniques), 50 ff.
   Kochi-Waza (hip techniques), 58 ff.
   Tandoku-Renshu (self-practice), 93–95
   Te-Waza (hand techniques), 69 ff.
Tai-Otoshi (body drop), 85–87
Tai-Sabaki (turns), 29–30
Tandoku-Renshu (self-practice)
   for Marote-Seinage, 93–95
Tate-Shiho-Gatame (lengthwise locking of the four quarters), 120–124
   escapes from, 123–124
Te-Waza (throw with hands), 69 ff.
   Ippon-Seoi-Nage (one-hand-over-the-shoulder), 69–70
   Marote-Seoi-Nage (two-arm shoulder), 71–73
   Tai-Otoshi (body drop), 85–87
Tomoe-Nage (circle throw), 149–151
Tsuri-Komi-Goshi (lift-pull-hip-throw), 78–80
Twisting body, 21
Uchi-Mata (inner thigh throw), 90–92
Ukemi (breaking fall) exercises, 32–48
Uki-Goshi (floating hip throw), 58–59
Warming-up exercises, 15–23
   back snake crawl, 23
   bending to the side, 16–17
   body bridge, 22
   loosening ankles, knees, neck, 16, 17, 18
   importance of, 15
   push-ups, 19
   rocking on front and back, 20
   stretching leg muscles, 18, 19, 20
   swinging and pivoting, 15
   twisting body, 21,
Wazi-Ari (half-point award), 156
Yoko-Shiho-Gatame (side-four-quarter hold), 113–118
   escapes from, 116–118
Zarai (sitting bow), 12–14